CUTE & CUDDLY
CROSS STITCH

CUTE & CUDDLY
CROSS STITCH

Gillian Souter

× × ×

David & Charles

A DAVID & CHARLES BOOK

First published in the UK in 2003

Text and designs Copyright © Gillian Souter 2003
Photography and layout Copyright © David & Charles 2003

Distributed in North America
by F&W Publications, Inc.
4700 East Galbraith Road
Cincinnati, OH 45236
1-800-289-0963

A catalogue record for this book is available from the British Library.

ISBN 0 7153 1228 6
Designed by Off the Shelf Publishing
and printed in Italy by Stige
for David & Charles
Brunel House   Newton Abbot   Devon

Executive Editor Cheryl Brown
Desk Editor Sandra Pruski
Executive Art Editor Alison Myer
Production Controller Ros Napper

Gillian Souter is the author of more than 20 books, including craft titles for both children and adults, but
this is her first cross stitch book based entirely on her own illustrations. Gillian was born in Scotland, moved
to Australia when young, and now lives in a beautiful coastal township in New South Wales.

David & Charles books are available from all good bookshops; alternatively you can contact our Orderline
on (0)1626 334555 or write to us at FREEPOST EX2110, David & Charles Direct, Newton Abbot, TQ12
4ZZ (no stamp required UK mainland).
Visit our website at www.davidandcharles.co.uk

CONTENTS

MUSINGS

XXX

You might wonder at the above heading, but the term
'introduction' seemed a trifle serious for the occasion.
This book is, after all, simply about cross stitching
things that make you want to smile and sometimes
even chuckle out loud.

As you've already opened this book, I'm most likely speaking to the converted, who know that cross stitching is one of the pleasures of life. It's relaxing, addictive, and unlike many other pleasures, quite harmless. The act of stitching is enjoyable in itself, so it's a bonus when you find designs that have lasting appeal and can be made into gifts that others will gladly receive. I hope there are many of those in *Cute & Cuddly Cross Stitch*.

If you pressed me for a definition of what makes something 'cute and cuddly', I'd mumble a few vague guidelines about baby animals, the occasional small child, and the need to tread a tightrope over the abyss of kitsch. The designs which follow are influenced by my fondness for children's books, a theme which has been played out in my previous cross stitch books of storybook characters. This fondness comes to the fore in the designs that tell a narrative: a chick hatches and leaves the nest, a hedgehog acquires a floral coat, the koala baby gets tangled in mum's knitting wool. Other images just raise questions: what are those mice celebrating and where's my invitation? Whoever told that chicken it should take up tennis? Undoubtedly, my idea of what is cute won't match everyone's, but I have a very special cute-ometer: a husband with a fine sense of humour who won't hesitate to say when he thinks I'm being too silly.

To balance the cute with the cuddly, I've included some slightly more realistic animal designs – a supping squirrel, a fairy penguin, a bicycling fox (just kidding!) – that appeal to anyone who has a love of the natural world. As well as being an enthusiastic cross-stitcher, I'm a keen hiker and a ramble is never perfect unless I've spotted a bit of cuddly fauna. I have yet to see a giant panda in the wild, with or without a picture book, but I can only hope.

Just because a design is quirky doesn't mean it can't be put to a practical use. I've included suggestions for an array of bags, holders, cards and whatnot, with full instructions for making them. There's plenty of room though for experimentation and substitution. Other shades and types of fabric can easily be used; just remember to recalculate the size of the finished design before you buy any fabric of a different count. Scraps of Aida or evenweave can be used to make cards or backed with fusible webbing and ironed onto all manner of things. A larger design can always be plundered for a small detail, particularly if you're short of time or thread!

Whatever the scale of the projects you undertake, I hope you enjoy stitching them, and I hope too that they will continue to draw a smile from you for many years afterwards.

A Few Techniques

✕ ✕ ✕

Cross stitch is one of the most popular
of crafts and is extremely simple to learn.
If you're new to this form of embroidery,
this section will give you the information
needed to work the projects in this book.
If you've been cross stitching for some time,
I'd recommend that you skip over it, as it's
a little bit on the dry side.

Reading the Charts

In cross stitch, a pattern is transferred from a charted design to a piece of unmarked fabric. The charts in this book are grids of squares with colours and some symbols. A key tells you which colour of DMC stranded cotton (floss) relates to which colour symbol on the chart. Working the design is simply a matter of stitching a series of crosses in the appropriate colour according to the arrangement on the chart.

Most designs also include backstitch, shown on the chart as thick coloured lines, and a few include French knots, shown as dots. Arrows indicate the centre of the design.

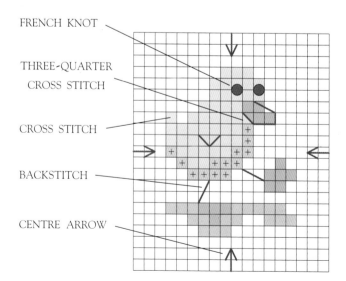

FRENCH KNOT

THREE-QUARTER CROSS STITCH

CROSS STITCH

BACKSTITCH

CENTRE ARROW

Fabric

Cross stitch fabrics are evenly woven, that is, they have the same number of threads over a given distance both vertically and horizontally. Aida fabric, formed with bands of threads, is often used. There are many types of fabric woven in single threads: these can be made of various fibres but they're referred to in this book as evenweave.

The size of each stitch is determined by the number of fabric threads over which you sew and by the number of bands or threads per inch of fabric (known as the fabric count). Most fabric counts are still given in inches, even in countries that have adopted the metric system. 26-count evenweave has twenty-six threads per inch of fabric and each stitch covers two threads (to prevent the embroidery thread gliding under a fabric thread) so there are thirteen stitches per inch. With 30-count evenweave, there are fifteen stitches per inch: the larger the fabric count, the smaller the stitches will be.

The instructions for each project specify the type of fabric used to stitch it and the amount of fabric required. When you choose a fabric with a different thread count, you will need to calculate what the size of the stitched design will be. Use the following rule: finished size equals the design stitch count divided by the fabric count and then divide by two if working with evenweave rather than Aida. Multiply the result by 2.5 to convert from inches into centimetres.

Fabrics for cross stitch are available in a wide range of colours, but unusual shades are often more expensive. If you can't find the shade you want, or if you have white or off-white fabric to spare, you could try tinting it yourself. Acrylic paint, when mixed with plenty of water to make a wash, can be brushed on to damp fabric. This will dry a slightly darker shade and can look a little blotchy, which looks fine as sky, for example. Do not use this method for a project that will need washing. For a more even colouring and for permanence, use a fabric dye, following the instructions on the packet.

Thread

All designs in this book have been stitched with DMC stranded cotton (floss). If you wish to use a different brand, match the colours in the pictures as closely as possible or create your own combinations afresh.

The six strands of the embroidery thread can be split into single strands, three lengths of double strands, or other combinations. The number of strands used depends on the count of your fabric. In general, using more strands will make your finished work more vivid, but if you use too many strands they will not fit neatly within the weave of the fabric. Most of the projects in this book are stitched with two strands for cross stitch and one for backstitch and French knots.

Equipment

Use a blunt needle such as a small tapestry needle that will not split the fabric threads. Match the size of the needle to the size of the hole: a size 26 needle is suitable for all of the projects in this book.

You will need two pairs of scissors: a small pair for trimming threads and a pair of shears for cutting the fabric.

If you are stitching a large design, or one that requires similar thread shades, your spare strands can easily become jumbled. To make a simple thread holder, cut a length of sturdy card and use a hole punch to cut holes at regular intervals. Mark the colour number and symbol alongside the hole and tie the threads on loosely.

A frame or embroidery hoop will help you to stitch evenly and prevent warping, but it is not necessary. I prefer simply to roll the fabric at either side. If you do choose to use a hoop, choose one which will fit the whole design, otherwise it may damage existing stitches.

There are lots of commercial products available to help you keep threads and projects in order. I keep my collection of stranded cottons (floss) in plain old manila folders, hooked onto spikes which I've snipped along the top. When there's only a bit of thread left, I wind it onto a cardboard bobbin. I have a stack of clear plastic trays (old developing trays for photographers) in which I keep all the materials I need for works in progress. Have fun finding your own particular methods!

Preparing to Stitch

If your fabric has a stubborn crease, steam press it before you start stitching. To prevent the fabric from fraying when cross stitching large projects, zigzag the edges on a sewing machine or simply use masking tape which can later be removed.

Locate the centre of the fabric by folding it in half and then in half again. If you are working on a large design, mark the centre with a pin and use a coloured thread to tack from side to side and from top to bottom, each time tacking through the centre mark. This should quarter your fabric. When you start cross stitching, make sure the centre of the design (indicated by arrows on the chart) matches the centre point of your fabric.

Check the project instructions regarding the position of the stitching on the fabric; if there are no specific instructions, orient the fabric to match the chart and stitch the

design in the centre. Count out from the centre point to where you want to start stitching.

Cut a length of embroidery thread, say 16in (40cm) long, and gently split it into the appropriate number of strands. Let the strands dangle and untwist.

Stitching

Thread the needle with the appropriate number of strands and bring it through the fabric, leaving ½in (1.5cm) of waste thread at the back. Hold this tail carefully and make sure that your first four or five stitches secure it, then trim any excess. The diagram below shows the back of the fabric with a secured tail.

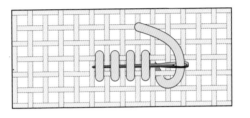

STARTING
(BACK VIEW)

FINISHING
(BACK VIEW)

CROSS STITCH

Stitch a series of diagonal bars running from left to right. Then, at the end of the row, return by stitching the top bars from right to left. Drop your needle to the bottom of the next row and repeat the process. Stitches in a sequence interlock, sharing holes with the neighbouring stitch.

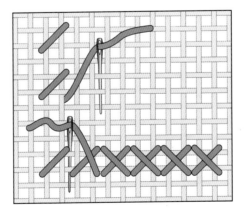

A ROW
OF CROSS
STITCHES

Remember, the number of threads crossed by a single stitch will depend on your fabric: on evenweave fabric, each stitch covers two threads, on Aida each stitch covers one band of threads.

Work horizontally rather than vertically and do not change directions; even though you may use more stranded cotton (floss), the result will look much neater.

Once you have stitched some crosses, use them as your reference point and count from them, rather than from the centre. On large projects, your tacked centre lines remain useful as a crosscheck that you are counting correctly. Complete each block of colour, jumping short distances where necessary, but always securing the thread at the back by running the needle under existing threads. If blocks are some distance apart, finish off the first and start afresh.

To finish off each section, run your needle through the back of four or five stitches and trim the stranded cotton (floss) close to the fabric.

THREE-QUARTER STITCH

Many of the charts contain some three-quarter stitches. These are indicated on the chart by a right-angled triangle and are usually found around the edges of a design. In this case, one diagonal of the cross stitch is formed in the usual way, but the second stitch is brought down into the central hole of linen, or into the centre of an Aida block.

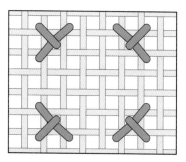

Where the chart indicates two different three-quarter stitches in the same square, you will need to decide which colour should predominate in the second diagonal.

BACKSTITCH

Many of the charts include backstitching to define outlines and provide detail. It is indicated by a solid line on the chart. Backstitch is always worked after cross stitching is completed and is worked in a continuous line. The method is best described in the diagram below.

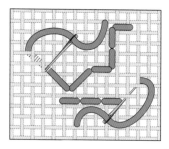

Backstitch can be worked as single stitches over one or two counts of fabric, or as longer stitches when working a cat's whisker or another such feature.

FRENCH KNOTS

This is a useful stitch for adding tiny features such as eyes. In this book they are usually worked with a single strand of stranded cotton (floss) and are shown on the chart as a small coloured dot.

To work a French knot, bring the needle up to the right side of the fabric, hold the thread down with your left thumb (if you are right-handed) and wind the thread around the needle twice or three times, depending on the size of knot you want. Still holding the thread taut, push the needle through to the back of the work, one thread or a part of a band away from the entry point. See the diagram below.

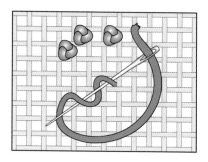

BLANKET STITCH

While this isn't a standard stitch in the cross stitch repertoire, it can be useful as a decorative edging that prevents fabric from fraying.

Start by bringing the thread out on the lower line shown in the diagram below. Re-insert the needle at position 1 at the upper line and out again at 2, keeping the thread under the needle point so a loop is formed.

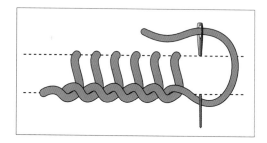

Extra Tips

It's important to keep your work as clean and fresh as possible. Don't leave unfinished work in an embroidery hoop for too long. When not in use, always secure the needle at the edge of the fabric to prevent ugly rust marks or damage to the fabric.

Do not fold work-in-progress; roll it in a layer of tissue paper. A sheet of acetate (available from art supply shops) offers good protection for a large project.

Cut your stranded cotton (floss), as you need it, into 16in (40cm) lengths. If you use longer strands they will start to fray after you've been cross stitching for a while.

If you are working a design with two strands, here is a useful tip: cut a long single strand, thread both ends through the needle and catch the end loop at the back on your first stitch to neatly secure the end.

As you stitch, the thread tends to twist. This may produce uneven stitches so, if it happens, let the needle dangle from the fabric so that the thread can unwind.

When moving from one area of a colour to another patch of the same colour, don't jump the thread across the back if the gap will remain bare. Such leaps will show through the fabric in the finished work.

If you make an error in counting, do not try to rescue the embroidery thread for reuse. Use a pair of small pointed scissors to snip misplaced stitches and carefully pull out the strands, then stitch correctly with a new piece of stranded cotton (floss).

Avoid the temptation to start or finish off with a knot; it will form a lump when the work is laid flat.

Finishing

It's almost impossible to keep a large cross stitch project clean. My personal nightmare is cat hairs so I always check the completed work closely for unwanted filaments. Most works will benefit from a gentle wash in lukewarm water with a mild detergent. Rinse it well and place the damp fabric on a clean white towel to dry on a flat surface. To iron, lay the work face down on a clean white towel, cover it with a clean cloth and then press.

Many of the projects suggested in this book require general sewing techniques such as hemming, seaming and using bias binding as edging. This isn't the place for a detailed explanation of such methods; if the instructions are unclear, you might do well to refer to a general guide to sewing techniques.

Framing

To frame a cross stitch work, the fabric first needs to be wrapped around a mount board and taped or laced in position. A professional framer can do this for you, or you can do it yourself. As a compromise, you could ask the framer to cut the mount board and backing board for you.

Mount board should be acid-free board of a colour that will not show through the fabric. It should be cut to fit inside the picture frame, allowing for the thickness of the fabric which will cover it.

Place the cut board on the back of the stitched work, ensuring it is centred. Starting from the centre of one of the longest sides, fold the excess fabric over onto the board, then pin through the fabric and into the edge of the board.

Check that the design is in the correct position, with no wrinkles, then proceed to tape or lace.

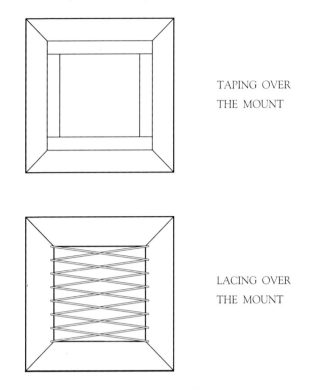

TAPING OVER
THE MOUNT

LACING OVER
THE MOUNT

If you opt for the taping method, use strong tape to secure two opposite flaps onto the back of the mount board. Fold the corners neatly and then tape the other two flaps. Remove the pins when taping is complete.

If lacing, work from the centre and lace two opposite flaps of fabric with long lengths of strong thread. Fold the corners neatly and then lace the other two flaps. Remove the pins when lacing is complete.

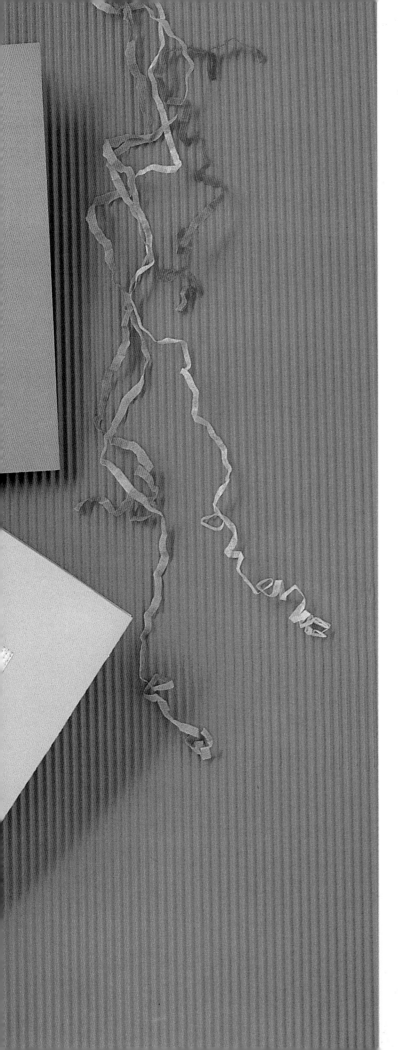

THE BEAR ESSENTIALS

*If there were a popular vote on cuteness,
bears would probably win the day.
Some particularly charming bears feature
in this set of cards for every occasion.
There are no fractional stitches so the
designs are very bearable to work!*

Bear Up! Get Well Card

DESIGN COUNT	53w 50h
FINISHED DESIGN SIZE	3¾ x 3½in (9.5 x 9cm)

MATERIALS

* White 14-count Aida, 6 x 6in (15 x 15cm)
* DMC stranded cottons (floss) as listed in the key
* Yellow card, 18¾ x 6¼in (48 x 16cm)
* Double-sided tape

1 Find the centre of the fabric and stitch the design following the chart on page 14. Use two strands of stranded cotton (floss) for cross stitch and one strand for backstitch.

2 Lightly score two lines on the card with a craft knife and fold to create three even panels. Trim a narrow strip off the left panel. Mark a 4 x 4in (10 x 10cm) window in the centre panel and cut it out with the craft knife.

3 Apply double-sided tape on the inside of the centre panel. Position the stitched work in the window and stick down the left-hand panel as a backing.

BEAR UP!

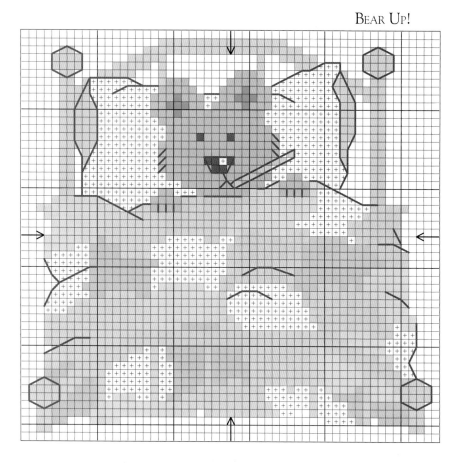

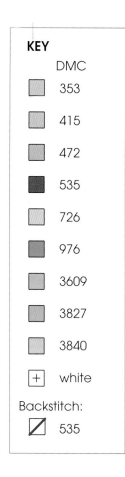

KEY

DMC

▨	353
▨	415
▨	472
▨	535
▨	726
▨	976
▨	3609
▨	3827
▨	3840
+	white

Backstitch:

◪	535

HAPPY BEAR-THDAY

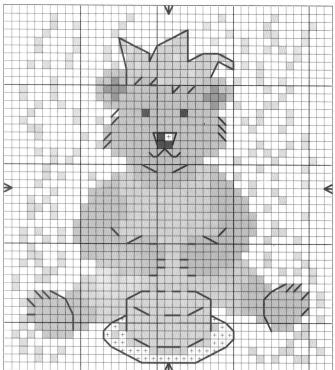

Happy Bear-thday Card

DESIGN COUNT	41w 44h
FINISHED DESIGN SIZE	3 x 3⅛in (7.5 x 8cm)

MATERIALS

* White 14-count Aida, 5 x 6in (12.5 x 15cm)
* DMC stranded cottons (floss) as listed in the key
* Green card, 16½ x 6½in (42 x 16.5cm)
* Double-sided tape

1 Find the centre of the fabric and stitch the design following the chart. Use two strands for cross stitch and one strand for backstitch.

2 Lightly score two lines on the card with a craft knife and fold to create three even panels. Trim a narrow strip off the left panel. Mark a 3 x 3¾in (8 x 9.5cm) window in the centre panel and cut it out with the craft knife.

3 Apply double-sided tape on the inside of the centre panel. Position the stitched work in the window and stick down the left-hand panel as a backing.

Baby Bear Card

DESIGN COUNT   41w 41h

FINISHED DESIGN SIZE   3 x 3in (7.5 x 7.5cm)

MATERIALS

* White 14-count Aida, 6 x 6in (15 x 15cm)
* DMC stranded cottons (floss) as listed in the key
* Orange card, 18¾ x 6¼in (48 x 16cm)
* Double-sided tape

1 Find the centre of the fabric and stitch the design following the chart. Use two strands for cross stitch and one strand for backstitch.

2 Lightly score two lines on the card with a craft knife and fold to create three even panels. Trim a narrow strip off the left panel. Use compasses to mark a circle with a diameter of 4in (10cm) in the centre panel. Cut out this window with the craft knife.

3 Apply small pieces of double-sided tape on the inside of the centre panel. Position the stitched work in the window and stick down the left-hand panel as a backing.

BABY BEAR

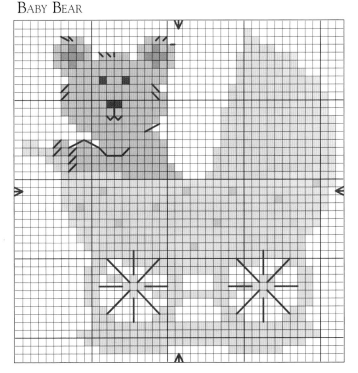

Snowbear Card

DESIGN COUNT   42w 50h

FINISHED DESIGN SIZE   3 x 3½in (7.5 x 9cm)

MATERIALS

* White 14-count Aida, 4½ x 5½in (11.5 x 14cm)
* DMC stranded cottons (floss) as listed in the key
* Purple card, 15 x 6¼in (37.5 x 16cm)
* Double-sided tape

1 Find the centre of the fabric and stitch the design following the chart. Use two strands for cross stitch and one strand for backstitch.

2 Lightly score two lines on the card with a craft knife and fold to create three even panels. Trim a narrow strip off the left panel. Sketch an oval measuring 3 x 3½in (7.5 x 9cm) on scrap paper and cut this out. Use this template to mark an oval window in the centre panel. Cut it out with the craft knife.

3 Apply small pieces of double-sided tape on the inside of the centre panel. Position the stitched work in the window and stick down the left-hand panel as a backing.

SNOWBEAR

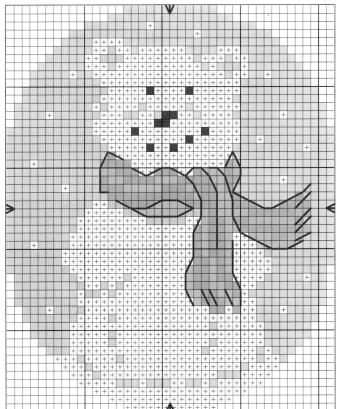

Leaping Sheep

✕ ✕ ✕

*Stitch a few gambolling sheep onto
your sheet set or duvet cover and you'll be
dreaming sweet dreams in no time.
There are no fractional stitches in these
designs and they are a good introduction
to stitching over waste canvas.*

Bed Linen Trim

DESIGN COUNT   22H (WIDTH IS ADAPTABLE)

FINISHED DESIGN SIZE   2in (5cm) HIGH

MATERIALS

* A strip of 11-count waste canvas, 3in (8cm) wide
* DMC stranded cottons (floss) as listed in the key
* A fine cotton sheet or duvet cover

1   Decide how wide you want the cross stitching to extend on the sheet. Cut a suitable sized strip of waste canvas and pin it in place along the top of the sheet. Secure the waste canvas with large tacking stitches.

2   Stitch the repeat trim design charted on page 18 in the centre of the waste canvas. Use three strands of stranded cotton (floss) for cross stitch and two strands for backstitch and French knots.

3   Remove the tacking threads. Dampen the canvas by pressing gently with a clean cloth or sponge. Remove the threads one at a time with a pair of tweezers. Press the work carefully.

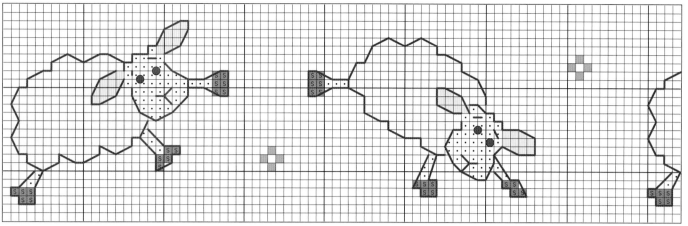

TRIM SHEEP

KEY

	DMC			DMC
U	318		-	3024
X	334			3348
S	451		·	white
	519			
	746		Backstitch:	
	948		/	451
			/	826
			French knots:	
			●	451

PILLOW SHEEP

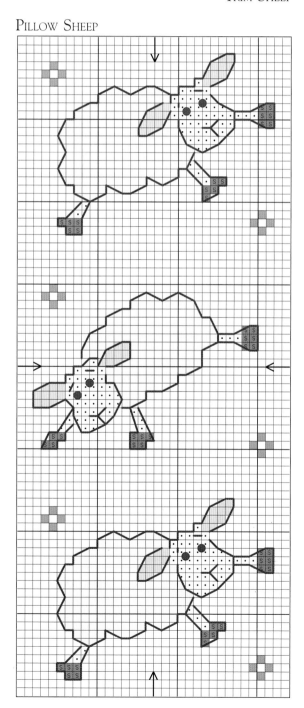

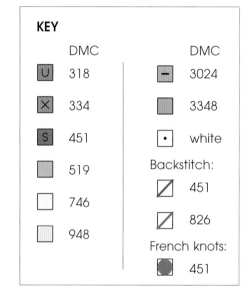

Pillow Case

DESIGN COUNT   30w 76h

FINISHED DESIGN SIZE   2¾ x 7in (7 x 17.5cm)

MATERIALS

* 11-count waste canvas, 4 x 8½in (10 x 22cm)
* DMC stranded cottons (floss) as listed in the key
* A fine cotton pillow case

1 Position waste canvas near the opening of the pillow case, with short edges top and bottom, and pin it in place. Secure the waste canvas with large tacking stitches.

2 Stitch the design on the right in the centre of the waste canvas. Use three strands of stranded cotton (floss) for cross stitch and two strands for backstitch and French knots.

3 Remove the tacking threads. Dampen the canvas by pressing gently with a clean cloth or sponge. Remove the threads one at a time with a pair of tweezers. Press the pillow case carefully.

Small Pyjama Satchel

DESIGN COUNT   87w 50h

FINISHED DESIGN SIZE   6¾ x 3⅞in (17 x 10cm)

MATERIALS

* 26-count white evenweave, 12¾ x 7½in (32 x 19cm)
* DMC stranded cottons (floss) as listed in the key
* Cover fabric, 12¾ x 20¾in (32 x 52cm)
* Lining fabric, 12¾ x 27½in (32 x 69cm)
* Thin wadding, 12¾ x 27½in (32 x 69cm)
* Ribbon; sewing thread

1   Orient the evenweave fabric so that the long edges are top and bottom and stitch the design charted below in the centre. Use two strands of stranded cotton (floss) for cross stitching and one strand for backstitch and French knots.

2   Lay the stitched evenweave on the cover fabric, right sides facing, with the top of the evenweave aligned with a short edge of the cover fabric. Sew a ³⁄₈in (1cm) seam.

3   Lay the stitched cover and the lining section togther, right sides facing, and place the thin wadding on top. Baste around the edges, then sew a ³⁄₈in (1cm) seam around all edges, leaving a gap for turning. Trim excess wadding and turn the work right side out.

4   With the cover face down, fold the bottom end (opposite the evenweave) up by 9in (23cm) to form a large pocket. Pin and then slipstitch one side of the pocket and then the other. Fold the decorated flap over and sew two ribbon bows on the bottom of the flap.

OVER THE GATE

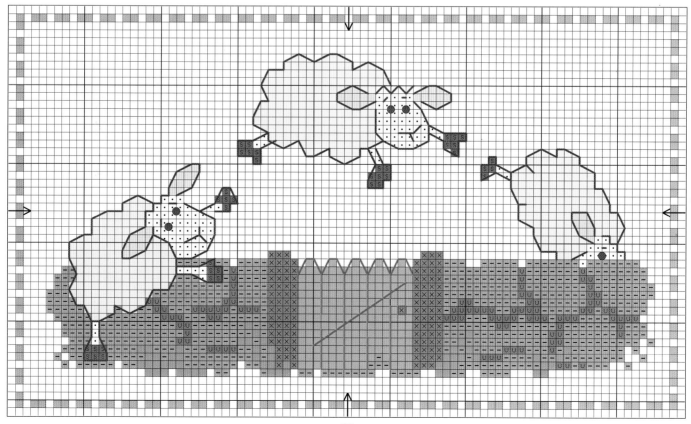

HEDGEHOG ROLL

✕ ✕ ✕

*Hedgehogs are often overlooked
by embroiderers, possibly because they
are cute but not-so-cuddly. This floral
hedgehog decorates a bathroom set, but he
would also be fun stitched on a T-shirt.*

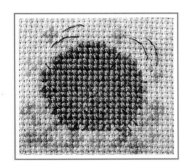

Trinket Pot

DESIGN COUNT   33w 33h

FINISHED DESIGN SIZE   2³⁄₈ x 2³⁄₈in (6 x 6cm)

MATERIALS

* White 14-count Aida, 3½ x 3½in (9 x 9cm)
* DMC stranded cottons (floss) as listed in the key
* Jar with minimum 2½in (6.5cm) diameter lid
* Double-sided tape
* Ribbon

1 Stitch the larger hedgehog design following the chart
on page 22. Use two strands of stranded cotton (floss) for
cross stitch. Use one strand for backstitch and French knots.

2 Wash and dry a suitable glass jar. Lay double-sided tape
on top and around the lid. Position the work over it.

3 Work around the fabric edges, snipping at intervals in
towards the lid. Press these darts onto the side of the lid,
then trim the excess. Stick more double-sided tape over
the darts and wrap a length of ribbon around it.

POT HEDGEHOG

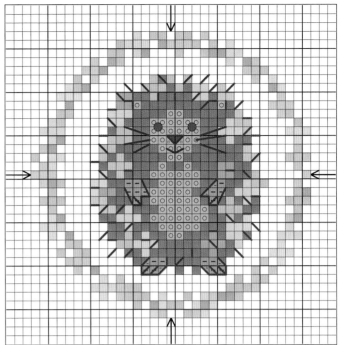

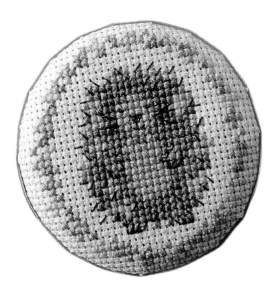

Towel Band

DESIGN COUNT 23h (width is adaptable)

FINISHED DESIGN SIZE 1⅝in (4cm)

MATERIALS

* White 14-count Aida band, 2in (5cm) wide
* DMC stranded cottons (floss) as listed in the key
* A hand towel
* Matching sewing thread

1 Cut a length of Aida band 2in (5cm) wider than your hand towel and stitch the figures following the chart below so they are evenly spaced. Use two strands of stranded cotton (floss) for cross stitch and one strand for backstitch and French knots.

2 Pin the Aida band onto the towel, turning the ends under neatly. Secure the Aida with small neat stitches.

KEY

	DMC		DMC
	211		3032
	353		3787
	472		3811
−	613	**Backstitch:**	
○	644	╱	3787
	744	**French knots:**	
	809	●	3787

TOWEL HEDGEHOG

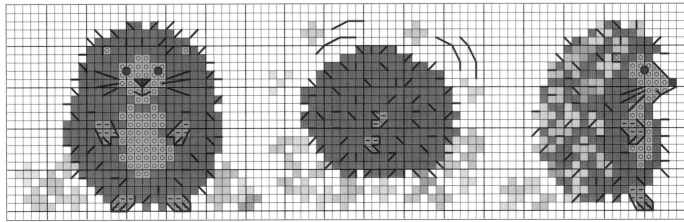

Balancing Acts

✕ ✕ ✕

*If life sometimes seems like a juggling act
here are a few designs to organise your
existence, balance the books and
seal your destiny!*

Bookmarks

DESIGN COUNT   TURTLE TOWER 29w 93h
                   MONKEY BUSINESS 25w 93h

FINISHED DESIGN SIZE   2 x 6⅝in (5 x 16.5cm)

MATERIALS

* Homespun 14-count Aida, 3 x 8in (8 x 20cm)
* DMC stranded cottons (floss) as listed in the key
* Coloured card, 2½ x 8in (6.5 x 20cm)
* Narrow ribbon

1 Orient the fabric to match the design. Find the centre of the fabric and stitch one of the designs on page 24. Use a single strand of stranded cotton (floss) for cross stitching the border; use two strands for the rest of the cross stitching. Use one strand for French knots and backstitch.

2 Trim the Aida fabric to leave one band of threads intact around the border cross stitches. Use a glue stick to secure the embroidery onto the coloured card.

3 Use a craft knife to make a small cut ½in (12mm) up from the base of the card. Thread a narrow ribbon through and secure it with an overhand knot. Trim ends.

Turtle Tower

Monkey Business

KEY for Turtle Tower

DMC

■	700
◉	702
+	704
■	3819

Backstitch:

◢	310

French knots:

●	310

KEY for Monkey Business

DMC

■	738
■	801
+	3824
■	3826

Backstitch:

◢	310

French knots:

●	310

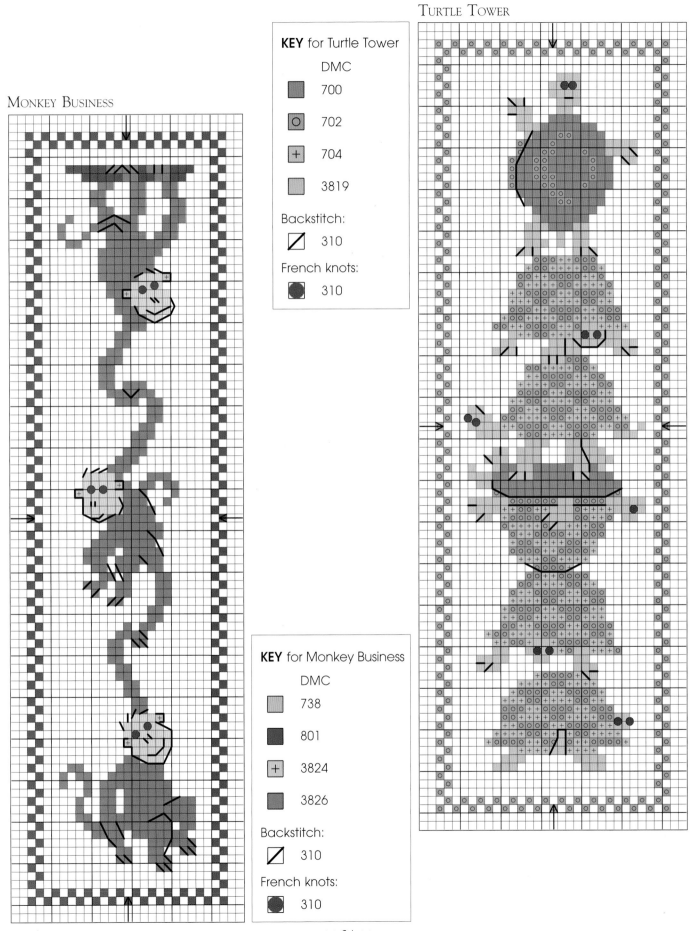

Sealed Paperweight

DESIGN COUNT   43W 43H

FINISHED DESIGN SIZE   2¾ x 2¾in (7 x 7cm)

MATERIALS

* White 16-count Aida, 4½ x 4½in (12 x 12cm)
* DMC stranded cottons (floss) as listed in the key
* Glass paperweight for embroidery

1 Find the centre of the Aida fabric and stitch the small design below. Use a single strand of stranded cotton (floss) for cross stitching the border in DMC 959; use two strands for the rest of the cross stitching. Use one strand for French knots and backstitch.

2 Centre the stitching over the paper or card template supplied with the paperweight and trim to fit.

3 Mount the work in the paperweight according to the manufacturer's instructions.

SEAL SALUTE

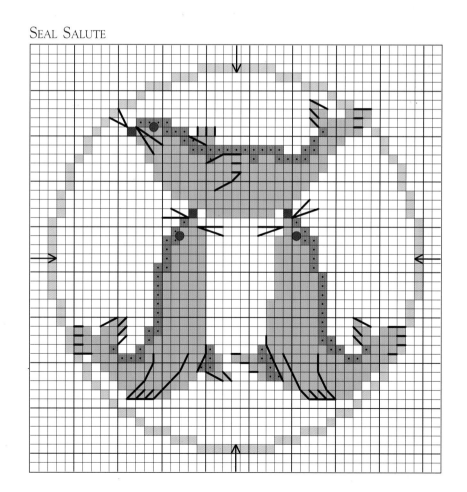

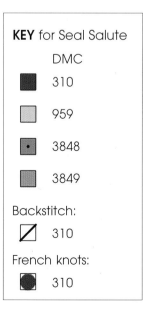

KEY for Seal Salute

DMC

■ 310

□ 959

▣ 3848

▨ 3849

Backstitch:

◪ 310

French knots:

● 310

Leaving the Nest

× × ×

*Welcome a new chick to the nest
with a charming card or a nursery frieze.
Remember to leave plenty of time to work
the backstitch or your chick may have
flown the nest!*

Nursery Frieze

DESIGN COUNT	268w 75h
FINISHED DESIGN SIZE	21 x 6in (53 x 15cm)

MATERIALS

* White 25-count evenweave, 27 x 12in (68 x 31cm)
* DMC stranded cottons (floss) as listed in the key
* Stiff white cardboard, 24 x 9in (61 x 23cm)
* Strong thread

1　Find the centre of the evenweave fabric and stitch the design following the charts on pages 28-30. Use two strands of stranded cotton (floss) for cross stitch. Use one strand for backstitch and French knots.

2　Position the white cardboard on the reverse of the work. Starting from the top centre, fold the fabric over the cardboard and pin it onto the board. Repeat this for each side, folding corners neatly.

3　Secure the fabric edges with long lacing stitches, working top to bottom and then side to side. Remove the pins. Tape a length of strong thread across the back for hanging.

Hatched Chick Card

DESIGN COUNT   48w 38h

FINISHED DESIGN SIZE   3½ x 2¾in (8.5 x 7cm)

MATERIALS

* White 28-count evenweave, 6½ x 5½in (16 x 14cm)
* DMC stranded cottons (floss) as listed in the key
* Pale card, 10 x 6in (25 x 15cm)
* Double-sided tape

1 Find the centre of the evenweave fabric and stitch the small design following the chart. Use two strands of stranded cotton (floss) for cross stitch. Use one strand for backstitch.

2 Lightly score a line down the centre of the card with a craft knife and fold it in half.

3 Trim ½in (12mm) around the stitched work and fringe the edges. Apply double-sided tape on the back of the work and stick it on the front of the card.

LEAVING THE NEST - CHART 1

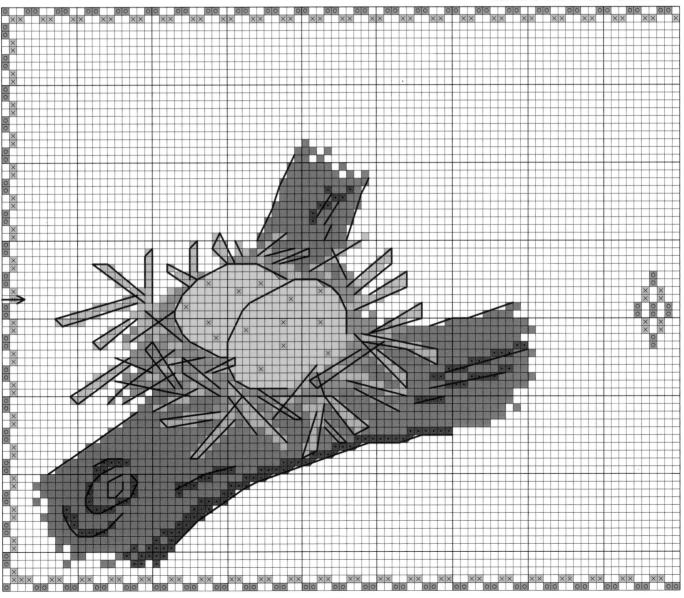

HATCHED CHICK

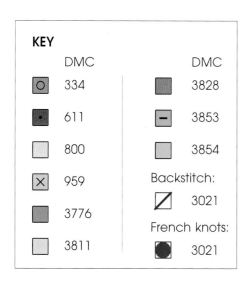

KEY

	DMC			DMC
⊙	334		▨	3828
⊡	611		–	3853
▢	800		▨	3854
×	959			
▨	3776		**Backstitch:**	
▢	3811		⊿	3021
			French knots:	
			●	3021

LEAVING THE NEST - CHART 2

KEY

	DMC			DMC
O	334		■	3828
■	611		−	3853
☐	800		☐	3854
✕	959			
■	3776	Backstitch:		
☐	3811	◹	3021	

French knots:

● 3021

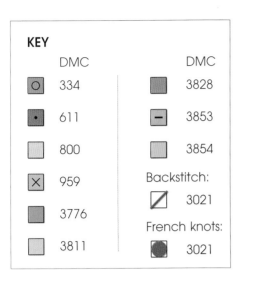
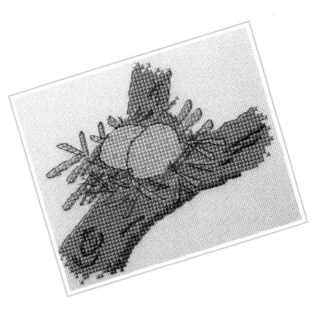

LEAVING THE NEST - CHART 3

Snacking Panda

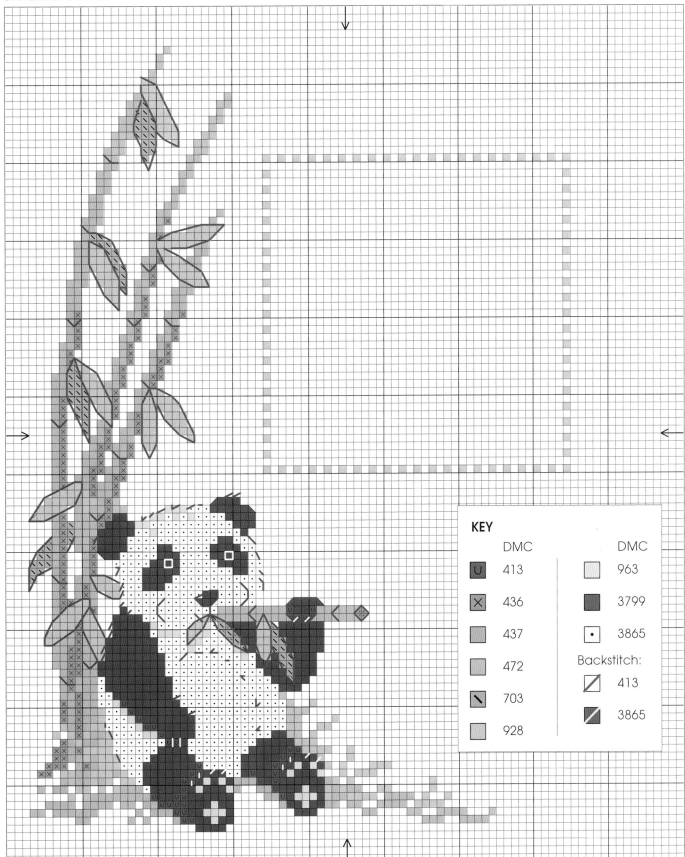

KEY

	DMC			DMC
U	413			963
✕	436			3799
	437		•	3865
	472			Backstitch:
╲	703		╱	413
	928		╱	3865

Panda Love

×××

There aren't that many pandas left in this world so a new panda is rather special - particularly to its mum. This photo frame and baby album are pretty special too.

Photo Frame

DESIGN COUNT   62w 101h

FINISHED DESIGN SIZE   4½ x 7¼in (11.5 x 18.5cm)

MATERIALS

* Green 28-count evenweave, 8½ x 10in (22 x 25cm)
* DMC stranded cottons (floss) as listed in the key
* Stiff cardboard, 6½ x 8in (16.5 x 20cm)
* Double-sided tape; PVA glue
* Felt, 6 x 7½in (15 x 19cm)

1   Orient the evenweave fabric to match the shape of the frame. Stitch the design in the centre of the fabric, following the snacking panda chart on page 31. Use two strands of stranded cotton (floss) for cross stitch and one strand for backstitch.

2   Position the work over the cardboard and pin it in place. Use a pin to mark each corner inside the stitched square.

Remove the work and cut out the window; it should be no more than 2¾in (7cm) square. Lay double-sided tape around the window and position the stitched work over the cardboard once more.

3 Apply PVA glue in a thin line within the window area. Snip the fabric in the centre of the square and then cut towards the window to form darts. Turn the darts over and tape them neatly onto the back of the card.

4 Turn the outside edges of the fabric over and secure them on the back of the frame with some more tape. Position a suitable photograph behind the window and tape it onto the back of the frame.

5 Glue a piece of felt over the back of the frame.

Baby's Album

DESIGN COUNT   62w 101h

FINISHED DESIGN SIZE   4½ x 7¼in (11 x 18cm)

MATERIALS

* Green 28-count evenweave, 26 x 15in (66 x 38cm)
* DMC stranded cottons (floss) as listed in the key
* A white 2-ring binder (A4 size)
* Sheets of thin card, 8¼ x 11in (21 x 28cm)
* Thin wadding
* Glue; tape
* Ribbon

1 Orient the evenweave fabric so the long edges are top and bottom. Measure 7in (18cm) in from the right edge; this is the centre point for stitching. Stitch the panda's bedtime by following the charts. Use two strands of stranded cotton (floss) for cross stitch and one strand for backstitch.

2 Cut a piece of thin wadding to size and glue it onto the front of the binder. Position the stitched fabric over the wadding and then wrap it around the binder, folding the edges over.

3 Secure the edges inside the binder with tape, starting at the spine. Mitre the corners neatly. Glue a sheet of thin card on the inside front and the inside back, covering the taped edges.

4 Cut a length of wide ribbon and glue it over the inside spine, then tie a bow on the outside spine. Punch holes in the remaining sheets of thin card and insert them in the binder as pages for the album.

PANDA'S
BEDTIME

KEY

	DMC
U	413
✕	436
	437
	472
\	703
	928
	963
<	964
	3761
S	3766
	3799
•	3865
+	white

Backstitch:

⟋	413
⟋	928
⟋	3865

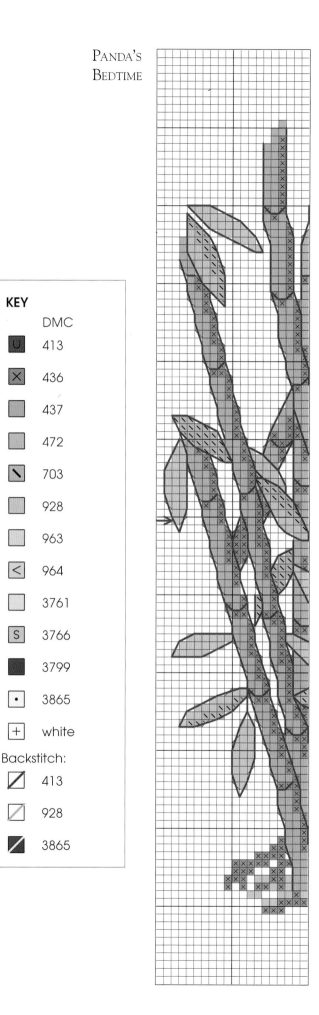

Elephantasy

× × ×

*Everyone has their dream home
and elephants are no exception.
You might like to replace the repeat pattern
with a "Home Sweet Home" motto using
the letters at the back of the book.*

Our House Sampler

DESIGN COUNT   130w 113h

FINISHED DESIGN SIZE   9¼ x 8in (23.5 x 20.5cm)

MATERIALS

* White 28-count evenweave, 16 x 14in (40 x 35cm)
* DMC stranded cottons (floss) as listed in the key
* Framing materials

1 Locate the centre of the evenweave fabric and fit it in
an embroidery frame if you wish. Stitch the design following the chart on pages 42-43, using two strands of stranded
cotton (floss) for all cross stitching. Use one strand for
backstitch and French knots.

2 Press the sampler carefully and frame it. There are tips
for framing in the Basic Techniques section at the begin-
ning of the book.

KEY

DMC

▨	211
▨	350
◣	414
▨	415
+	554
O	704
T	911
✕	912
–	945
▨	954
U	977
Z	3341
▨	3747
▢	3823
●	3826
▨	3839
▨	3856
•	white

Backstitch:
◿	414
◿	912
◿	3826

French knots:
▨	414

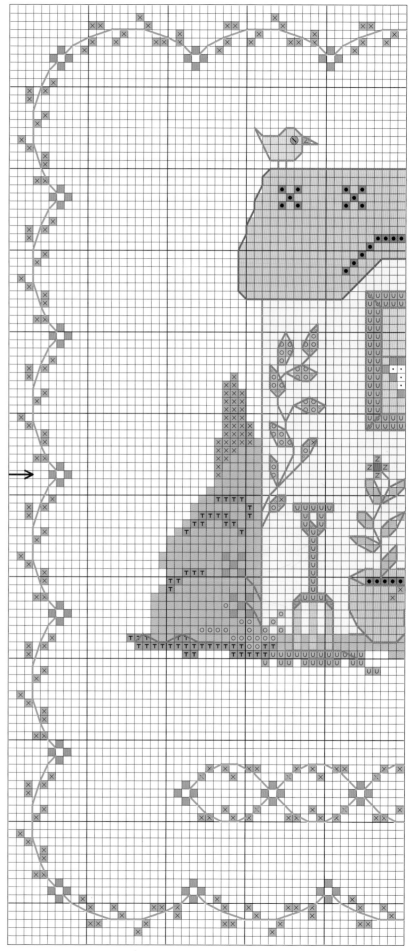

Ducklings on Parade

✕ ✕ ✕

Ducklings – like babies and toddlers
– are very impressionable and these
useful gifts for you to stitch are sure
to imprint a little of your love on
any hatchling.

Pot Trim

DESIGN COUNT   26H (WIDTH IS ADAPTABLE)

FINISHED DESIGN SIZE   1⅞in (4.6cm) HIGH

MATERIALS

* Cream 14-count Aida band, 2in (5cm) wide
* DMC stranded cottons (floss) as listed in the key
* A round container
* Sewing thread

1 Measure the circumference of your container by wrapping a tape measure around it. Cut a piece of Aida band ⅞in (2cm) longer than this measurement.

2 Stitch the ducklings design charted overleaf. Use two strands of stranded cotton (floss) for cross stitch. Use one strand for backstitch and French knots. Start in the centre and work outwards, repeating the design as necessary.

3 Fold the band in half with right sides facing and sew the ends together with a ³⁄₈in (1cm) seam. Turn the band the right way out and slip it over the container.

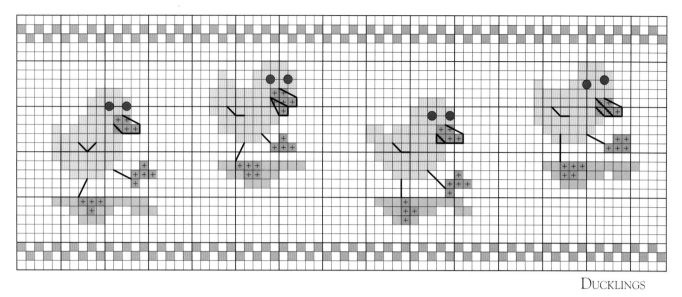

DUCKLINGS

Tidy Bag

DESIGN COUNT   78w 86h

FINISHED DESIGN SIZE   5½ x 6⅛in (14 x 15.5cm)

MATERIALS

* Rustic 14-count Aida, 25½ x 10½in (64 x 26.5cm)
* DMC stranded cottons (floss) as listed in the key
* 29in (72cm) of cloth tape or ribbon
* Sewing thread

1 Zigzag the edges of the Aida fabric to prevent fraying. Sew a ⅞in (2cm) hem at both of the narrow ends. Stitch the design on the opposite page so that the top of the design starts 1⅝in (4cm) below a hemmed edge. Use two strands of stranded cotton (floss) for cross stitch. Use one strand for backstitch and French knots.

2 On each hemmed edge of the fabric, mark two points, each 3⅜in (8.5cm) in from the sides. To form the handles, cut two pieces of tape, each 14½in (36cm) long and sew a ⅞in (2cm) hem at each end. Pin each end of one tape onto the marked points on a hemmed edge of the fabric and sew it securely in place. Repeat for the other handle, sewing it onto the other hemmed edge.

3 Fold the fabric in half with wrong sides facing and the hemmed edges aligned. Pin the two layers of fabric at each side, at a point 2in (5cm) up from the folded edge. Turn the front flap over and the bottom flap under so that the design is now inside the bag and there is a valley fold in the base. Sew a ⅞in (2cm) seam along the two sides.

4 Turn the completed bag right side out. Place a plastic bag inside as a disposable liner.

Baby's Bib

DESIGN COUNT   61w 37h

FINISHED DESIGN SIZE   4⅞ x 3in (12.2 x 7.4cm)

MATERIALS

* Bone 25-count evenweave, 8 x 10in (20 x 25cm)
* DMC stranded cottons (floss) as listed in the key
* Lining fabric, 8 x 10in (20 x 25cm)
* Bias binding, 70in (180cm)
* Sewing thread

1 Draw the bib shape on paper, using the pattern on page 108 as a guide; note that the dashed line denotes a fold. Make sure the neck is large enough to fit the baby comfortably. Mark the bib shape on the evenweave fabric.

2 Stitch the girl with her toy (part of the larger design) on the lower half of the evenweave fabric. Use two strands of stranded cotton (floss) for cross stitch. Use one strand for backstitch and French knots.

3 Cut the evenweave and the lining fabric to shape. Baste the edges of the two layers together. Trim the outside edges with folded bias binding. Cut a 1yd (1m) length of bias binding and pin it around the neckline so that the ties are of even length. Starting at one end, sew along the folded bias binding, continuing around the neckline to finish at the other end.

KEY

	DMC		DMC		DMC		DMC
■	310	▨	704	▨	3839		
✕	434	▨	726	+	3853		
▨	436	•	945	−	3854		
O	702	U	3838				

Backstitch:

⧄ 310

French knots:

● 310

GIRL & DUCKLINGS

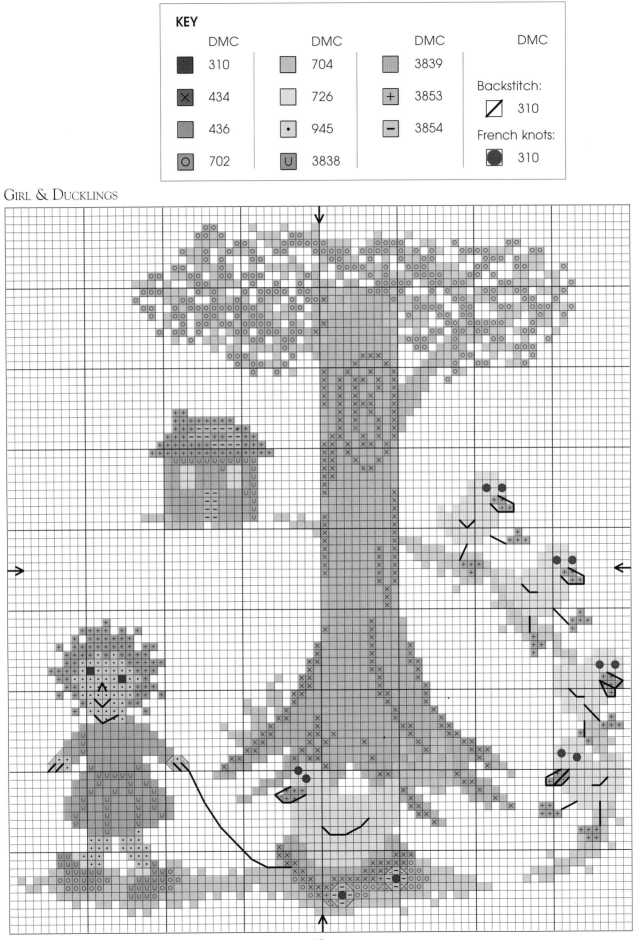

ANIMALIA

✕ ✕ ✕

*Some animals gain extra points on the
cuteness scale when they're in company.
There are no fractional stitches in
this assortment of animàlia, making the
individual designs ideal for children and
beginners to stitch.*

Counting Sampler

DESIGN COUNT	183W 189H
FINISHED DESIGN SIZE	11½ x 12in (29 x 29.5cm)

MATERIALS

* White 16-count Aida, 20 x 20in (50 x 50cm)
* DMC stranded cottons (floss) as listed in the key
* Framing materials

1   Locate the centre of the Aida fabric and then fit the
fabric in an embroidery frame if you wish. Stitch the design
following the chart on pages 46-49, using two strands of
stranded cotton (floss) for all cross stitching. Use one strand
for backstitch and French knots.

2   Wash and press the sampler carefully and then frame
it. There are tips for framing on page 11.

KEY

	DMC		DMC		DMC		DMC
▦	209	▦	726	▦	3607		Backstitch:
▦	310	▦	741	+	3839	◹	310
▦	350	▦	959	▦	3846		French knots:
✕	701	▦	977	○	3851	●	310
▦	704	▦	3340				

Animalia - chart 1

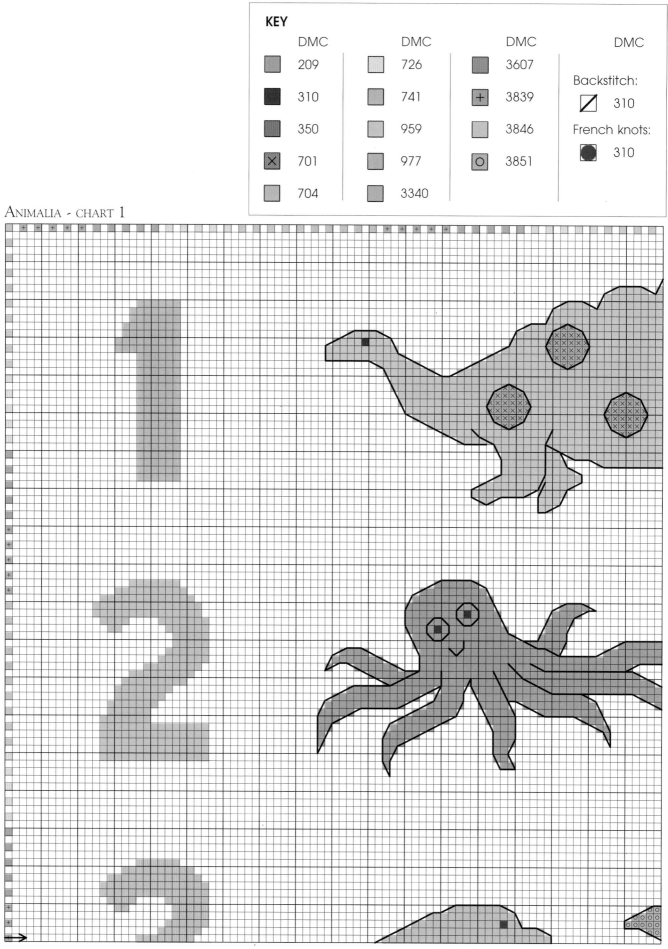

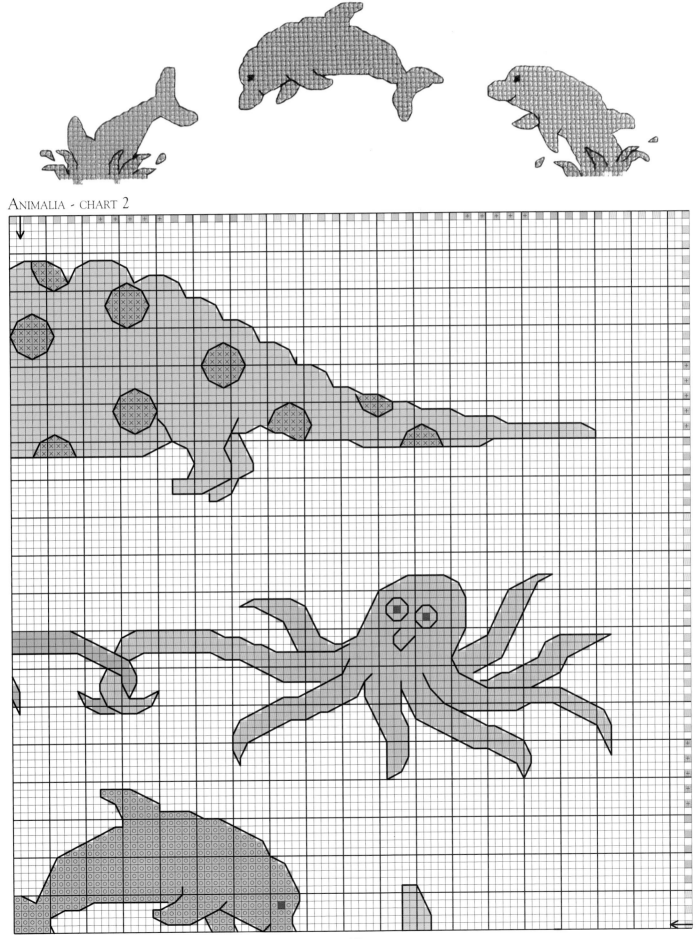

ANIMALIA - CHART 2

Animalia - chart 3

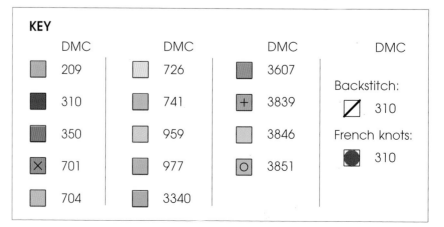

KEY

	DMC		DMC		DMC	DMC
	209		726		3607	Backstitch:
	310		741	+	3839	◹ 310
	350		959		3846	French knots:
✕	701		977	○	3851	● 310
	704		3340			

Decorative Trim

DESIGN COUNT   132w 24h

FINISHED DESIGN SIZE $8^7/_8$ x $1^5/_8$in (22.5 x 4cm)

MATERIALS

* White 15-count Aida band, 2in (5cm) wide
* DMC stranded cottons (floss) as listed in the key
* A pencil case at least 9in (23cm) wide
* Sewing thread

1   Measure the width of the pencil case. Cut a piece of Aida band $^7/_8$in (2cm) longer than this measurement.

2   Starting at the centre of the band, stitch the line of snails from charts 4 and 5. Use two strands of stranded cotton (floss) for cross stitch and one strand for backstitch and French knots.

3   Handsew the stitched work onto the pencil case, turning the ends of the Aida band under neatly.

SQUIRREL SUPPER

✕ ✕ ✕

Every squirrel knows that a lukewarm
cup of tea is not worth an acorn.
Make sure your pot stays snug with
this tea-cosy and a set of leafy mats.

Tea-cosy

DESIGN COUNT   99w 98h

FINISHED DESIGN SIZE   7 x 7in (18 x 18cm)

MATERIALS

* Green 28-count evenweave, 24 x 14in (60 x 35cm)
* DMC stranded cottons (floss) as listed in the key
* Lining fabric, 24 x 14in (60 x 35cm)
* Thin wadding, 24 x 14in (60 x 35cm)
* Ribbon, 4in (10cm)

1 Measure your teapot and, if necessary, adjust the following dimensions to fit. Cut the evenweave fabric into two 12 x 14in (30 x 35cm) pieces. Trace the pattern that appears on page 109 onto paper and, adding a ³/₈in (1cm) seam allowance all around, mark this shape onto both pieces of evenweave fabric with tailor's chalk.

2 Stitch the design on page 52 so that the bottom of the design starts 1in (2.5cm) from the base of an evenweave section. Use two strands of stranded cotton (floss) for cross stitch and one strand for backstitch. Continue stitching the background florets at regular intervals to fill the tea-cosy shape. You might also wish to stitch florets on the even-weave section that will form the back of the tea-cosy.

SQUIRREL SUPPING

3 Cut both the evenweave sections to shape. Cut two matching pieces of lining fabric and two of thin wadding. Compile the first section: stitched fabric face up, then lining fabric, and finally wadding on top. Pin these together and machine sew the bottom seam.

4 Turn the section right side out, with wadding between lining and evenweave and pin edges. Machine around the curved edge to secure the layers. Trim and zigzag the raw

edge to prevent fraying. Complete the second section in the same way.

5 Lay the two sides of the cosy together, with right sides facing. Fold a short piece of ribbon and pin it on, so that the two raw edges are aligned with the top edge of the cosy. Baste the pieces together around the curved edge, then machine sew just inside the basting stitches. Turn the finished cosy right side out.

Leaf Coasters

WOODLAND LEAVES

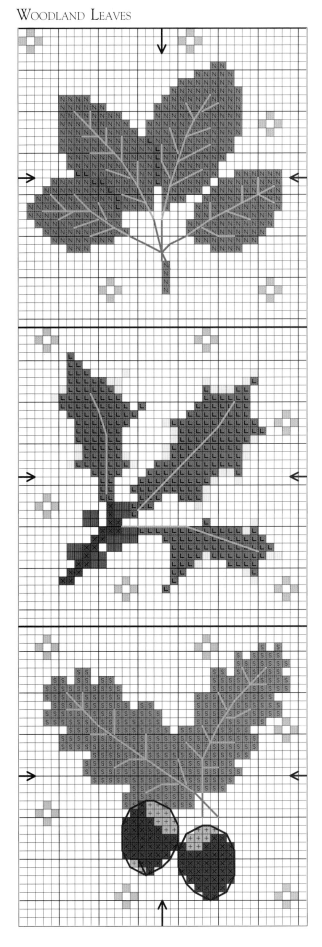

DESIGN COUNT   36w 36h

FINISHED DESIGN SIZE   2½ x 2½in (6.5 x 6.5cm)

MATERIALS

* Green 28-count evenweave, 5 x 5in (13 x 13cm)
* DMC stranded cottons (floss) as listed in the key
* Backing fabric, 5 x 5in (13 x 13cm)
* Thin wadding, 5 x 5in (13 x 13cm)
* Bias binding or ribbon, 15in (38cm)

1   The above measurements allow for a single coaster; increase them accordingly for the number you wish to make. On each square of evenweave fabric mark a circle with a 4in (11.5cm) diameter, using compasses.

2   Stitch one of the three woodland leaf designs using the chart on the right. Use two strands for cross stitch and one strand for backstitch. Continue stitching the background florets at regular intervals to fill the marked circle.

3   Cut a 5in (13cm) square of backing fabric and thin wadding and lay the evenweave on top, with cross stitching face up. Pin the layers together and baste them with stitches ¼in (5mm) in from the marked circle.

4   Trim around the circle and bind the raw edges with folded bias binding or satin ribbon.

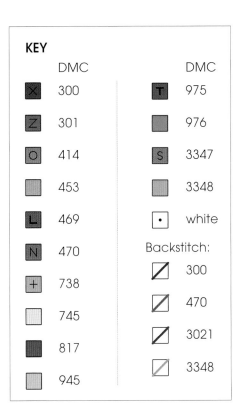

KEY

	DMC		DMC
X	300	T	975
Z	301		976
O	414	S	3347
	453		3348
L	469	•	white
N	470		Backstitch:
+	738	╱	300
	745	╱	470
	817	╱	3021
	945	╱	3348

FAERY FRIENDS

✕ ✕ ✕

*Every stitcher knows that there's a
mischievous goblin whose sole delight is to
waylay embroidery scissors and favourite
needles. Here are some magical friends to
take the cross out of cross stitching.*

Thread Holder

DESIGN COUNT	40w 60h
FINISHED DESIGN SIZE	2⁷⁄₈ x 4¼in (7.25 x 11cm)

MATERIALS

* Antique white 28-count evenweave, 16 x 8in
  (40.5 x 20cm)
* DMC stranded cottons (floss) as listed in the key
* Lining fabric, 16 x 8in (40.5 x 20cm)
* Ribbon
* Sewing thread

1   Orient the evenweave fabric so that the long edges are
at top and bottom. Mark a point 2¾in (7cm) in from the
right-hand edge and vertically central; this is the centre
point for the cross stitch.

2   Stitch the mermaid design centred on your mark, following the chart on page 56. Use two strands of stranded
cotton (floss) for cross stitch and one strand for backstitch
and French knots.

3 Orient the lining fabric so that the long edges are top and bottom and lay some ribbon at least 20in (51cm) long across the fabric so that one raw ribbon edge is aligned with the centre of the left fabric edge. An inch (2.5cm) in from these raw edges, sew the ribbon onto the lining with a few stitches.

4 Place a pencil to the right of the stitching and pin the ribbon down 1in (2.5cm) from the stitching. Remove the pencil and sew at the pinned point to create a loop of ribbon. Repeat this three times to create four ribbon loops. Secure the ribbon 1in (2.5cm) further along, this time without the pencil, so that it lies flat.

5 Repeat step 4 twice so that you have three sets of four loops. Lay the beribboned lining and the cover together with right sides facing. Sew a ³⁄₈in (1cm) seam around the edges, leaving an opening for turning. Trim the corners and turn the project right side out.

6 Insert skeins of cotton or floss for your current project and fold the holder in thirds so that the cross stitching is on the front. You might wish to sew on a snap fastener to keep the holder closed.

FLOSSY MERMAID

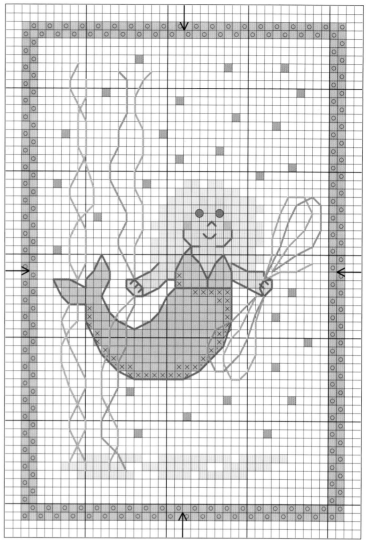

PIN ELF

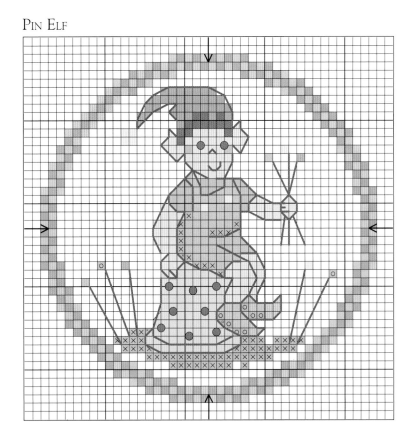

KEY

DMC		DMC	
⊙	209		3348
	211		3828
	415		3854
✕	471	**Backstitch:**	
	727	◹	209
	760	◹	413
	809	◹	471
	948	◹	809
		French knots:	
		●	413

Pin Cushion

DESIGN COUNT 42W 42H

FINISHED DESIGN SIZE 3 x 3in (7.75 x 7.75cm)

MATERIALS

* Antique white 28-count evenweave, 5 x 5in (12 x 12cm)
* DMC stranded cottons (floss) as listed in the key
* Backing fabric, 5 x 5in (12 x 12cm)
* Polyester fibre filler
* Cord (could be covered with ribbon to match set)
* Sewing thread

1 With long running stitches, mark a circle with a diameter of 4in (10cm) in the centre of the evenweave fabric.

2 Stitch the elf design in the centre of the evenweave fabric, following the chart found above. Use two strands of stranded cotton (floss) for cross stitch and one strand for backstitch and French knots.

3 Lay the two pieces of fabric together with right sides facing and sew around the marked circle, leaving a small opening for turning. Trim corners and turn right side out.

4 Insert the filler so that the seam is quite smooth. Sew the cord over the seam so that both ends are pushed into the opening, sewing the opening closed to complete.

Needle Case

DESIGN COUNT   40w 40h

FINISHED DESIGN SIZE   2⅞ x 2⅞in (7.25 x 7.25cm)

MATERIALS

* Antique white 28-count evenweave, 8¼ x 4½in (21 x 11cm)
* DMC stranded cottons (floss) as listed in the key
* Lining fabric, 8¼ x 4½in (21 x 11cm)
* White felt, 6¾ x 3¼(17 x 8cm)
* Narrow ribbon
* Sewing thread

1 With long running stitches, mark a rectangle on the evenweave fabric, ⅜in (1cm) in from each edge. Locate a point centred vertically and 2¼in (5.5cm) in from the right edge; this is the centre point for the cross stitching.

2 Stitch the fairy design, following the chart on this page. Use two strands of stranded cotton (floss) for cross stitch and one strand for backstitch and French knots.

3 Lay the felt on the right side of the lining fabric and sew the two together with a row of stitches down the centre. Lay this section felt side up and place a 12in (30cm) length of ribbon so that each edge lies in the centre of a short side of the lining fabric, with raw edges aligned.

4 Now lay the embroidered section on top, right side touching the felt, and sew around the running stitches, leaving an opening for turning. Trim the corners and turn the needle case right side out.

5 Sew the opening closed. Snip the ribbon in half, fold the needle case and tie the ribbons in a bow.

NEEDLE FAIRY

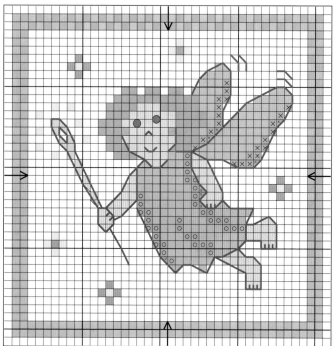

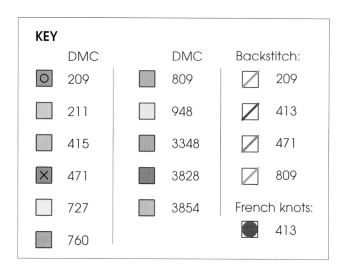

KEY

	DMC		DMC	Backstitch:	
O	209		809	◪	209
	211		948	◪	413
	415		3348	◪	471
✕	471		3828	◪	809
	727		3854	French knots:	
	760			●	413

SCISSORS GNOME

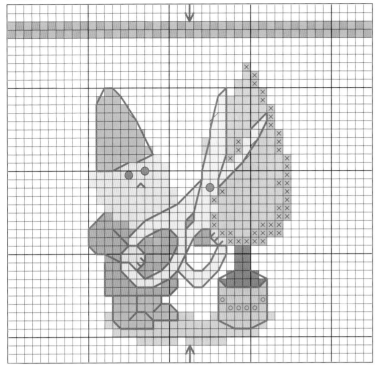

PATTERN FOR
SCISSORS KEEP

Scissors Keep

DESIGN COUNT	45w 39h
FINISHED DESIGN SIZE	3¼ x 2¾in (8 x 7cm)

MATERIALS

* Antique white 28-count evenweave, 5 x 8in (13 x 20cm)
* DMC stranded cottons (floss) as listed in the key
* Lining fabric, 8 x 5in (20 x 13cm)
* Narrow ribbon
* Sewing thread

1 Trace the pattern for the scissors keep onto tracing paper and cut out the template. Cut the evenweave fabric into two equal pieces, 5 x 4in (13 x 10cm) in size. In the centre of one piece, sew a series of running stitches around the paper template.

2 Cross stitch the gnome design within the marked area, so that the border at the top of the design is just inside the straight row of running stitches. Use two strands of stranded cotton (floss) for cross stitch and one strand for backstitch and French knots.

3 Lay the two pieces of evenweave fabric together, right sides facing, and sew around the curved line of running stitches. Trim ⅜in (1cm) outside the seam and turn the section right side out.

4 Cut the pattern twice from the lining fabric, adding a ¼in (6mm) allowance all around. Sew the lining pieces together around the curved edge, allowing a ⅜in (1cm) seam. Cut two 6in (15cm) lengths of ribbon.

5 Place the lining section inside the outer casing and fold the raw edges under at the opening. Slip the two pieces of ribbon between inner and outer sections and handsew the lining onto the outer section. Now insert the scissors and tie the ribbons into a bow.

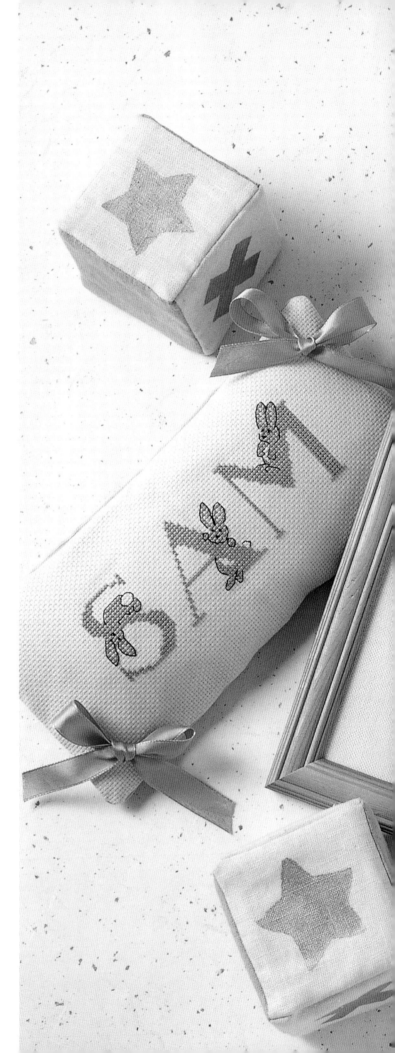

FUNNY BUNNY

✕ ✕ ✕

*The mischievous rabbit has a
long and well-recorded history,
from Peter Rabbit to Bugs
Bunny. Here are another twenty-
six to add to the list.*

Alphabet Sampler

DESIGN COUNT   198w 134h

FINISHED DESIGN SIZE   14$\frac{1}{8}$ x 9$\frac{1}{2}$in (35.5 x 24cm)

MATERIALS

* Sand 28-count evenweave, 22 x 18in (55 x 45cm)
* DMC stranded cottons (floss) as listed in the key
* Framing materials

1 Locate the centre of the evenweave fabric and fit fabric in an embroidery frame if you wish. Stitch the design
following the chart on pages 62-63, using two strands of
stranded cotton (floss) for all cross stitching. Use one strand
for backstitch and French knots.

2 Press the sampler carefully and frame it. There are tips
for framing on page 11.

NOTE: These letters can also be stitched as initials or a
name, on any number of gift items.

KEY

DMC
- 422
- 471
- 722
- 754
- 3371
- ⋅ white

Backstitch:
- ╱ 3371

French knots:
- ● 3371

PARTY MICE

✕ ✕ ✕

Who says mice don't know how to have a good time? These revelling rodents will undoubtedly lend a party atmosphere to any occasion you might be celebrating.

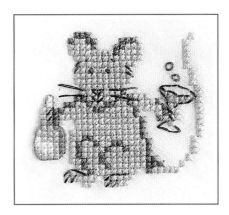

Tablecloth

DESIGN COUNT	130w 130h
FINISHED DESIGN SIZE	10 x 10in (25 x 25cm)

MATERIALS

* White 26-count evenweave, 36 x 36in (90 x 90cm)
* DMC stranded cottons (floss) as listed in the key
* Satin bias binding, 146in (365cm)

1 Zigzag the edges of the evenweave fabric to prevent fraying. Mark the centre of the fabric with a knotted loop of thread; this corresponds to the + mark on the chart on page 66. Stitch the first section of the design, using two strands of stranded cotton (floss) for cross stitch and one strand for backstitch and French knots.

2 Turn this book round 90 degrees so that the pattern is sideways. Stitch the next section of the design, substituting a different pair of colours for the ribbons: the darker shade in each pair is used to backstitch around the ribbon. Refer to the miniature picture on page 66 as a guide.

DANCING MICE   NOTE: + MARKS CENTRE OF FABRIC

3 Repeat step 2, once again substituting the colours for the ribbon. Repeat a final time to complete the last quarter of the full design.

4 Finish the tablecloth by sewing a length of folded satin bias binding around the edges.

KEY					
	DMC		DMC	Backstitch:	
O	208		415	◻	208
	210	U	726	◻	351
—	351		727	◻	413
	353	✕	958	◻	726
	413		964	◻	958
+	414	•	white	French knots:	
				●	413

Party Napkins

DESIGN COUNT   APPROXIMATELY 30W 30H

FINISHED DESIGN SIZE   3 x 3in (7 x 7cm)

MATERIALS

* 11-count waste canvas, 6 x 6in (15 x 15cm)
* DMC stranded cottons (floss) as listed in the key
* Four white cotton napkins, 10in (26cm) square

1 If you can't source plain white napkins, buy some strong cotton fabric, cut four 11in (28cm) squares and hem the edges. Fold each napkin twice so that creases mark it into four quarters.

2 Cut four pieces of waste canvas, each 4in (10cm) square. Lay an open napkin on the table, right side up, with a corner at top and bottom. Baste a piece of waste canvas onto the lower quarter.

3 Stitch one of the mice designs from the chart below. Use three strands of stranded cotton (floss) for cross stitch and two strands for backstitch and French knots.

4 Remove the basting threads and dampen the canvas with a cloth. Slowly pull out the strands of the waste canvas, one at a time. When you have stitched each design on a different napkin, carefully press them.

NAPKIN PARTY MICE

PUSS-IN-BOOTS

× × ×

*Kittens and columbines are an
irresistible combination. Here they
decorate three cushions made with
patchwork and appliqué techniques.*

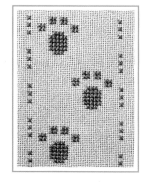

Kitten Cushion

DESIGN COUNT   98w 98h

FINISHED DESIGN SIZE   7 x 7in (18 x 18cm)

MATERIALS

* Beige 28-count evenweave, 10 x 10in (25 x 25cm)
* DMC stranded cottons (floss) as listed in the key
* Cushion fabric, 29½ x 14½in (75 x 37cm)
* Lining fabric, 14½ x 14½in (37 x 37cm)
* A cushion pad or filler; sewing thread

1   Stitch the puss-in-boots design centred on the
evenweave fabric, following the chart on page 70. Use two
strands of stranded cotton (floss) for the cross stitch and
one strand for backstitch. Trim the work to a square
measuring 8½in (22cm).

2   Cut four strips of cushion fabric, each measuring 3¾ x
14½in (9.5 x 37cm). Lay one strip on an edge of the stitched
work, right sides facing, and sew a ³⁄₈in (1cm) seam. Repeat with the remaining three strips. Fold the strip ends to
create a neat mitre at each corner. Baste and sew each
mitre, then trim and press the seams.

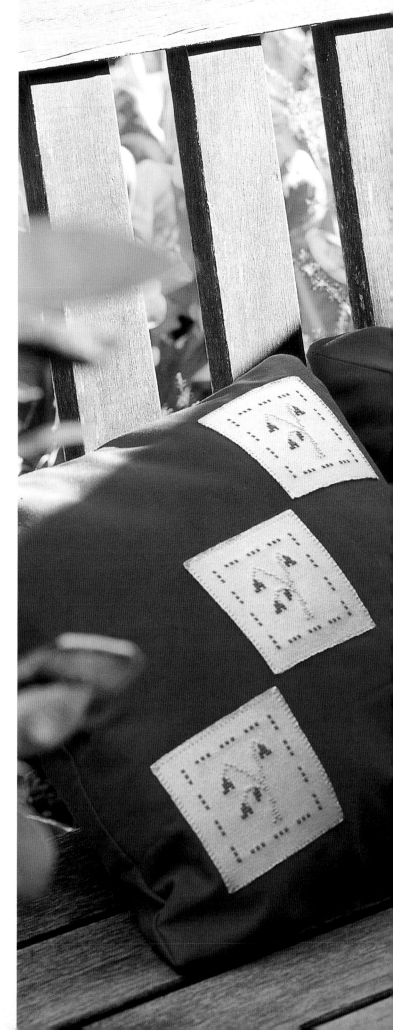

PUSS-IN-BOOTS

3 Line this front section with white lining fabric, basting the layers around the edges. Cut a piece of cushion fabric for the back. Lay front and back sections together, right sides facing, and sew a ³⁄₈in (1cm) seam around three sides. Trim excess fabric at the corners and turn right side out. Insert a cushion pad and slipstitch the opening closed.

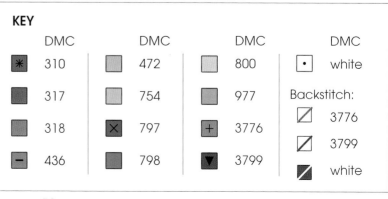

KEY							
	DMC		DMC		DMC		DMC
✱	310		472		800	·	white
	317		754		977		Backstitch:
	318	✕	797	+	3776	╱	3776
	436		798	▼	3799	╱	3799
						╱	white

Pawprint Cushion

DESIGN COUNT   26W 183H

FINISHED DESIGN SIZE   1⅞ x 13in (5 x 33cm)

MATERIALS

* Beige 28-count evenweave, 3¼ x 15in (8 x 38cm)
* Cushion fabric, 29 x 14½in (75 x 37cm)
* Lining fabric, 14½ x 14½in (37 x 37cm)
* A cushion pad or filler; sewing thread

1 Stitch the pawprint design on the evenweave fabric, starting ¾in (2cm) from the top of the strip and repeating the chart so the columbines are stitched three times. Use two strands of stranded cotton (floss).

2 Cut a 4¾ x 14½in (12 x 37cm) strip of cushion fabric and sew this on the stitched work, right sides facing, with a ⅜in (1cm) seam along one side. Cut 8 x 14½in (21 x 37cm) of cushion fabric and sew this piece, likewise, onto the other side of the stitched work. Press the seams.

3 Follow the instructions for step 3 on page 70.

Columbine Cushion

DESIGN COUNT   33W 32H

FINISHED DESIGN SIZE   2⅜ x 2⅜in (6 x 6cm)

MATERIALS

* Beige 28-count evenweave, 12 x 4in (30 x 10cm)
* Cushion fabric, 29 x 29in (75 x 75cm)
* Fusible webbing; sewing thread
* A cushion pad or filler

1 Cut three 4in (10cm) squares from evenweave. Stitch the columbine design on each piece, following the chart on the right and using two strands of stranded cotton (floss). Iron a piece of fusible webbing on the back of each piece and trim each to 3¼in (8cm) square.

2 Cut two 14½in (37cm) squares of cushion fabric. Arrange the stitched squares on the right side of the front cushion section and iron them in position. Sew around the edge of each square in blanket stitch, using two strands of DMC 3782 stranded cotton (see page 10).

3 Lay front and back cushion sections together, right sides facing, and sew a ⅜in (1cm) seam around three sides. Trim excess fabric at the corners and turn right side out. Insert a cushion pad and slipstitch the opening closed.

PAWPRINTS

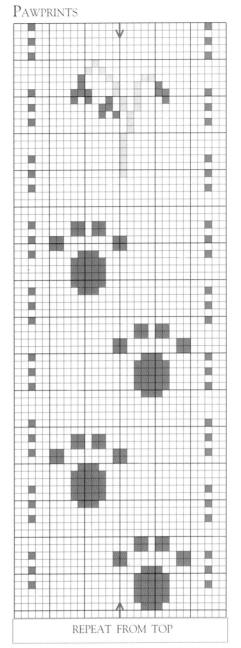

REPEAT FROM TOP

COLUMBINE

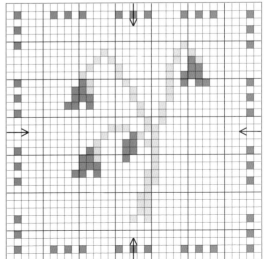

Penguin Noel

✕ ✕ ✕

Share a unique Christmas with
Penguin Noel, a quirky character
with a decidedly festive approach
to everyday activities.

Santa Noel Card

DESIGN COUNT   50w 40h

FINISHED DESIGN SIZE $3^5/_8$ x $2^7/_8$in (9 x 7.5cm)

MATERIALS

* Green 14-count Aida, 6 x 6in (15 x 15cm)
* DMC stranded cottons (floss) as listed in the key
* Red card, 6 x 15in (15 x 37.5cm)
* Double-sided tape

1 Stitch the design of Noel sledding following the chart on page 74. Use two strands of stranded cotton (floss) for cross stitch and one strand for backstitch and French knots.

2 Lightly score two lines on the card with a craft knife and fold to create three even panels. Trim a narrow strip off the top panel. Sketch an oval measuring $4^1/_8$ x $3^1/_8$in (10.5 x 8cm) on scrap paper and cut this out. Use this template to mark an oval window in the centre panel. Cut it out with the craft knife.

3 Apply double-sided tape on the inside of the centre panel. Trim the Aida fabric to 5 x $4^1/_2$in (12.5 x 11cm). Position the stitched work in the window and stick down the top panel as a backing.

Noel Sledding

Noel's Tree Card

DESIGN COUNT   45w 45h

FINISHED DESIGN SIZE   3¼ x 3¼in (8.2 x 8.2cm)

MATERIALS

* Red 14-count Aida, 5 x 5in (12.5 x 12.5cm)
* DMC stranded cottons (floss) as listed in the key
* Green card, 5 x 15in (12.5 x 37.5cm)
* Double-sided tape

1 Stitch the design of Noel decking the tree following the chart opposite. Use two strands of stranded cotton (floss) for cross stitch and one strand for backstitch and French knots.

2 Lightly score two lines on the card with a craft knife and fold to create three even panels. Trim a narrow strip off the top panel. Use compasses to mark a 3½in (9cm) diameter circle on the centre panel. Cut out this window with the craft knife.

3 Apply small pieces of double-sided tape onto the inside of the centre panel. Trim the Aida fabric to a 4¼in (11cm) square. Position the stitched work in the window (note that you can choose which way the card will open) and stick down the top panel as a backing.

Noel Decking

Noel's Decorations

DESIGN COUNT	NOEL FISHING 40w 40h
	NOEL'S GIFT 40w 40h

FINISHED DESIGN SIZE   3 x 3in (7.5 x 7.5cm)

MATERIALS FOR EACH DECORATION

* Red or green 14-count Aida, 5 x 5in (12 x 12cm)
* DMC stranded cottons (floss) as listed in the key
* Stiff cardboard, 4 x 4in (10 x 10cm)
* Red or green felt, 4 x 4in (10 x 10cm)
* Double-sided tape; ribbon

1 Stitch the design in the centre of the Aida fabric, following one of the charts on this page. Use two strands for cross stitch and one strand for backstitch and French knots.

2 Use compasses to draw a 3¼in (83mm) diameter circle on stiff cardboard. Cut out the card circle. Trim the embroidered Aida to an inch (2.5cm) around the border.

3 Lay strips of double-sided tape across the back of the embroidery. Centre the card circle carefully and stick it in place. Snip darts every ³⁄₈in (1cm), turn them over and stick them down neatly on the back of the card.

4 Cut a 9in (23cm) length of ribbon and tape the ends onto the back of the card to form a hanging loop. Mark and cut a circle of felt with a diameter of 3¾in (9cm). Use double-sided tape to stick the covered card on the felt.

NOEL FISHING

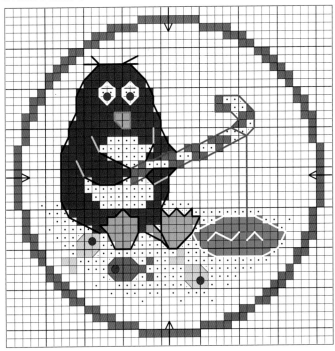

NOEL'S GIFT

KEY

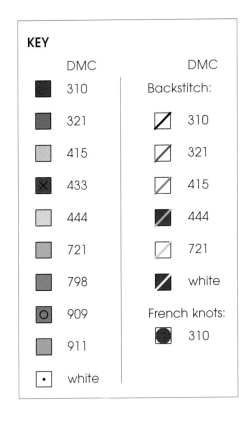

	DMC		DMC
■	310		Backstitch:
■	321	◻	310
◪	415	◻	321
✕	433	◻	415
◩	444	◪	444
◩	721	◻	721
◩	798	◪	white
○	909		French knots:
◩	911	●	310
·	white		

Noel's Christmas Stocking

DESIGN COUNT   MAIN DESIGN 50w 50h

FINISHED DESIGN SIZE   4½ x 4½in (11.5 x 11.5cm)

MATERIALS

* Blue 11-count Aida, 20 x 13in (50 x 35cm)
* DMC stranded cottons (floss) as listed in the key
* Blue lining fabric, 20 x 13in (50 x 35cm)
* Bias binding; sewing thread

1 Enlarge the stocking pattern on page 109 to twice its current size, using a photocopying machine or by rescaling the pattern. Cut out a paper template and use this to mark two shapes on the Aida fabric with tailor's chalk.

2 Stitch the design in the lower section of one Aida piece, as shown in the photograph opposite, following the chart below. Use three strands for cross stitch and two strands for backstitch and French knots.

3 Cross stitch two bands of snowflakes across the top section, spaced 1¾in (4.5cm) apart. You might want to cross stitch a child's name in this space, using the alphabet chart on page 111.

4 Cut the lining fabric into two pieces, each 10 x 13in (25 x 35cm). Lay the stitched work and a lining section with right sides together and sew a ½in (1.5cm) seam across the top edge. Turn the piece the right way out, baste the fabrics together along the raw edge and trim the lining fabric to match the Aida. Line the other piece of Aida in the same way.

5 Baste the front and back of the stocking together and finish the raw edges with bias binding, forming a hanging loop at the top right corner.

SNOWFLAKES

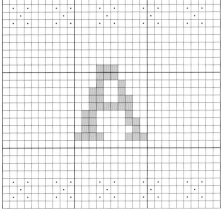

NOEL SINGING

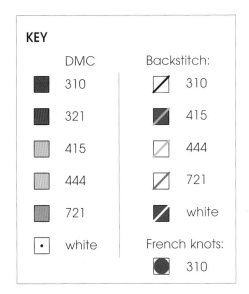

KEY

	DMC	Backstitch:	
■	310	⊿	310
■	321	◪	415
■	415	⬚	444
■	444	◹	721
■	721	◪	white
•	white	French knots:	
		●	310

SOMETHING FISHY

✕ ✕ ✕

*Not many people can claim to have
cuddled a fish, so it's possible that this
subject is simply a red herring.
Regardless, here are some useful
items for a trip to the pool or beach.*

Beach Towel Trim

DESIGN COUNT   23H (WIDTH IS ADAPTABLE)

FINISHED DESIGN SIZE   2¹⁄₈in (5.3cm) HIGH

MATERIALS

- A strip of white 11-count Aida, 3in (8cm) wide
- DMC stranded cottons (floss) as listed in the key
- A plain towel
- Bias binding; sewing thread

1 Cut the strip of Aida 2in (5cm) wider than your towel
and stitch the swish fish design following the chart on pages
80-81. The design is continuous so you can repeat it as
required at either end. Use three strands of stranded
cotton (floss) for cross stitch and one strand for backstitch.

2 Sew a length of bias binding along both edges of the
Aida strip and then sew the band onto the towel, turning
the ends under neatly.

Key Ring

DESIGN COUNT   17w 45h

FINISHED DESIGN SIZE   1¼ x 3¼in (3 x 8cm)

MATERIALS

* White 14-count Aida, 2¼ x 7½in (6 x 19cm)
* DMC stranded cottons (floss) as listed in the key
* Ribbon
* A metal keyring

1 Crease the strip of Aida fabric in half and stitch the fishy duo design in the centre of one half, following the chart on the right. Use two strands of stranded cotton (floss) for all cross stitching and one strand for backstitch.

2 Fold the Aida strip so the back of the cross stitching is concealed. Cut a 4in (10cm) length of ribbon, slip it through the metal ring and tuck the ribbon ends well into the folded Aida strip. Pin to hold it in place.

3 Secure the edges with blanket stitch (refer to page 10), using two strands of DMC 996 stranded cotton (floss).

FISHY DUO

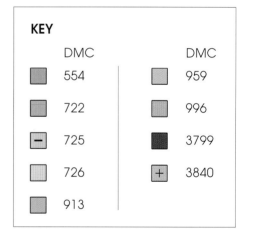

KEY

	DMC		DMC
	554		959
	722		996
−	725		3799
	726	+	3840
	913		

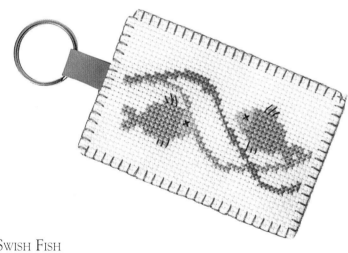

SWISH FISH

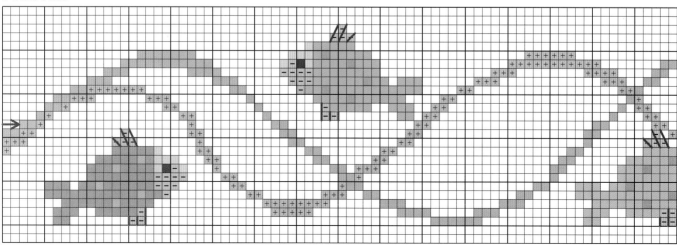

Swim Swag

DESIGN COUNT   115w 101h

FINISHED DESIGN SIZE   8¼ x 7¼in (21 x 18.5cm)

MATERIALS

* White 28-count evenweave, 10 x 9in (25 x 23cm)
* DMC stranded cottons (floss) as listed in the key
* Cover fabric, 26¾ x 13¾in (68 x 35cm)
* Lining fabric, 26¾ x 13¾in (68 x 35cm)
* Clear medium-weight vinyl, 12 x 16in (30 x 40cm)
* Fabric tape, 8½ft (2.5m)
* Velcro tape
* Snap fasteners; sewing thread

1 Stitch the fishbowl design in the centre of the evenweave fabric, following the chart on pages 82-3. Use two strands of stranded cotton (floss) for cross stitch and one strand for backstitch and French knots.

2 Back the stitched evenweave with lining fabric (not listed above) and pin the panel on the right side of the cover fabric so that the top is 2¼in (5.5cm) from one of the short edges. Secure the edges of the panel with blanket stitch (refer to page 10), using two strands of DMC 996 stranded cotton (floss).

3 Cut the clear vinyl into two 12 x 8in (30 x 20cm) pieces and make up each of the two pockets as follows. Round the corners on one short end. Fold up the other end by 4½in (12cm). Starting at the fold, bind up one side, around the curved flap and down the other edge with fabric tape. Sew two snap fasteners in place to hold the flap closed.

4 Position the pockets on the right side of the lining fabric, 3in (7.5cm) down from each short end, so that both flaps point inwards. Sew them in place, stitching along each side and inside the flap fold.

5 Cut two 12in (30cm) lengths of fabric tape for the towel straps. Turn each of the raw ends over and hem them (or dip ends in PVA glue). On one end of each strap, sew a 2in (5cm) strip of Velcro tape on the wrong side.

6 Position each strap so that the non-Velcro end is 1½in (4cm) below the base of a pocket corner. Secure in position with two rows of stitches. Sew 1in (2.5cm) pieces of Velcro tape at matching positions below the second pocket, making sure they are suitable partners for the Velcro on the straps.

7 Cut two 18in (46cm) lengths of fabric tape for the shoulder straps. Lay one strap on the right side of the lining fabric, so that the raw ends extend ½in (1cm) or so beyond the short end of the lining fabric and are spaced 7in (18cm) apart. Arrange the other strap on the other end of the lining fabric and baste both straps in place.

8 Pin the cover section and lining section together with right sides facing and then sew a ³⁄₈in (1cm) seam around the edges, leaving a 6in (15cm) gap for turning. Turn the swag right side out and handsew the opening closed.

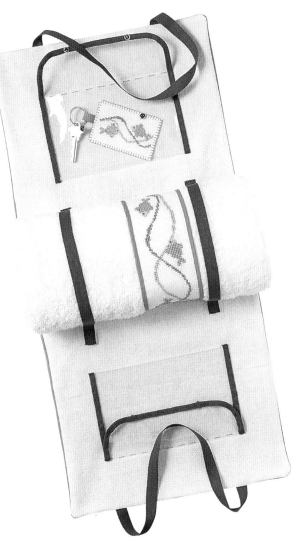

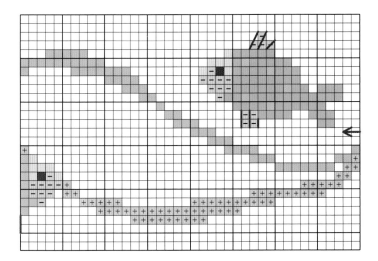

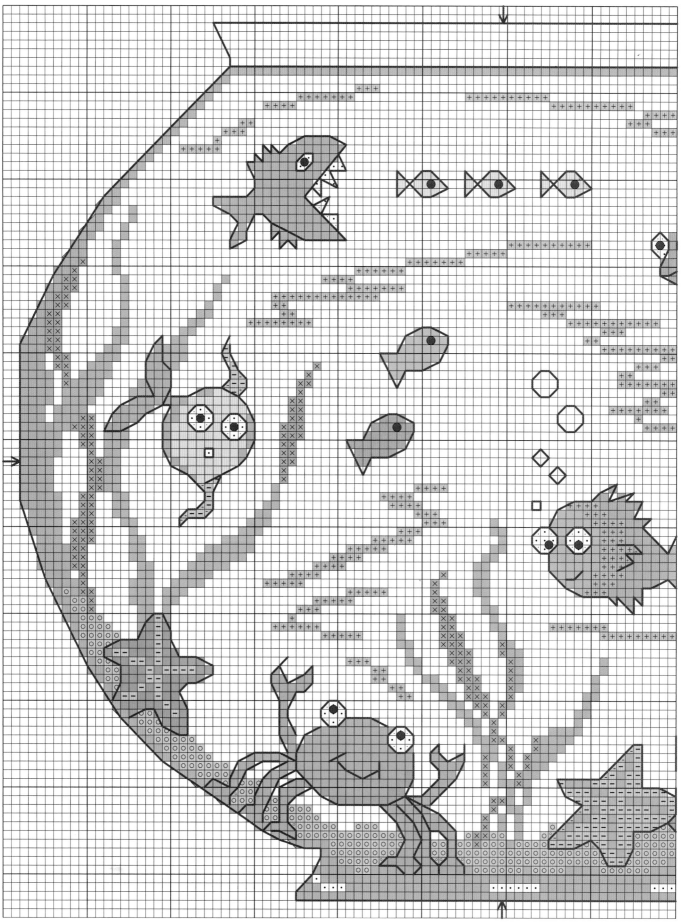

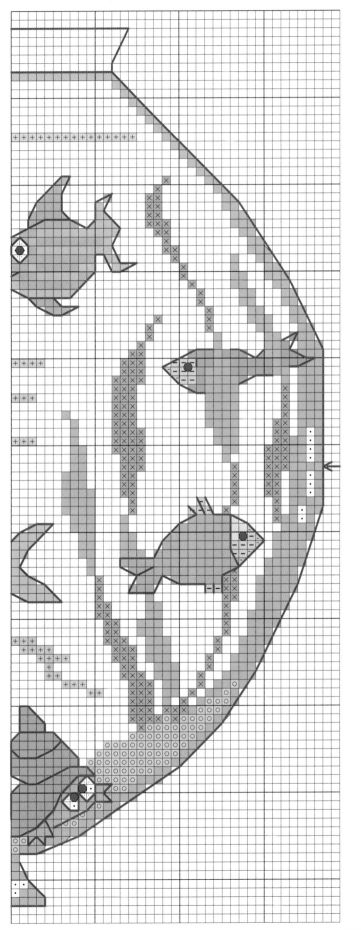

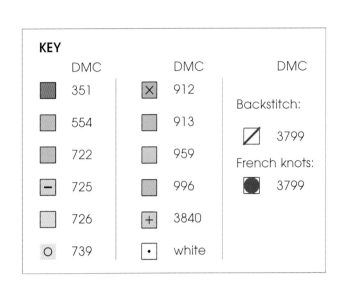

KEY

	DMC		DMC		DMC
▨	351	✕	912		Backstitch:
▨	554	▨	913	▱	3799
▨	722	▨	959		French knots:
−	725	▨	996	●	3799
▨	726	+	3840		
O	739	•	white		

COOL CRITTERS

× × ×

*There's not a lot to distract the eye
in the extreme north and south of
the planet, but what there is has a definite
charm. Here are some ice-bound inhabitants,
framed with two unusual techniques.*

Spatter Frame

DESIGN COUNT   50W 74H

FINISHED DESIGN SIZE 3⅝ x 5¼in (9 x 13.25cm)

MATERIALS

* Blue 28-count evenweave, 7 x 9in (18 x 23cm)
* DMC stranded cottons (floss) as listed in the key
* White card, 5 x 7in (13 x 18cm)
* Wooden frame with opening 5 x 7in (13 x 18cm)
* Acrylic paints; semi-gloss varnish

1 Orient the fabric so the narrow edges are top and bottom and stitch the penguin design in the centre, following the chart on page 86. Use two strands of stranded cotton (floss) for cross stitch and one strand for backstitch.

2 Apply a coat of light blue paint to the frame, giving it a second coat if necessary to achieve an even colour.

3 Dip an old toothbrush in white paint and run your finger across the bristles, testing the results on paper before spattering the frame. When dry, apply a coat of varnish.

4 Cut a piece of stiff white card to fit inside the frame. Lay this on the back of the stitched fabric, fold the edges over and tape them onto the back. Fit into the frame.

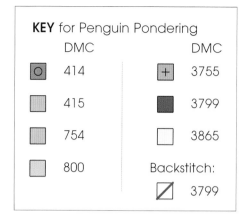

KEY for Penguin Pondering

	DMC		DMC
O	414	+	3755
	415		3799
	754		3865
	800	Backstitch:	
		⧄	3799

PENGUIN PONDERING

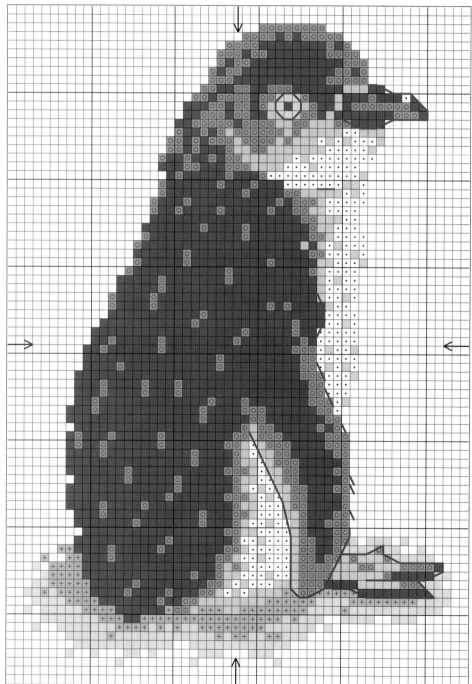

Limed Frame

DESIGN COUNT   80w 48h

FINISHED DESIGN SIZE   5 x 3in (12.5 x 7.5cm)

MATERIALS

* Blue 32-count evenweave, 7 x 9in (18 x 23cm)
* DMC stranded cottons (floss) as listed in the key
* White card, 5 x 7in (13 x 18cm)
* Wooden frame with opening 5 x 7in (13 x 18cm)
* Acrylic paint; semi-gloss varnish
* Plaster filler
* Sandpaper

1   Orient the fabric so the long edges are top and bottom and stitch the design in the centre, following the chart below. Use two strands of stranded cotton (floss) for cross stitch and one strand for backstitch.

2   Apply a coat of light blue paint to the frame, giving it a second coat if necessary to achieve an even colour.

3   Add a little water to a small amount of plaster filler and mix it to a smooth paste. Rub the paste on the frame with a circular movement, using a rag or your forefinger, then wipe it across the grain of the wood with a spatula. Allow the filler to dry.

4   Sand the filler with a piece of medium-fine sandpaper, to reveal the paint underneath but do not remove all the filler. Wipe with a dry cloth and apply a coat of semi-gloss varnish.

5   Cut a piece of stiff white card to fit inside the frame. Lay this on the back of the stitched fabric, fold the edges over and tape them onto the back. Fit into the frame.

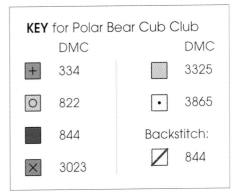

KEY for Polar Bear Cub Club			
	DMC		DMC
+	334	▨	3325
O	822	·	3865
■	844		Backstitch:
✕	3023	╱	844

POLAR BEAR CUB CLUB

Fit & Furry

✕ ✕ ✕

*Not everything that's cute and
cuddly is shapeless and overweight!
Here are some inspiring projects for
when you're feeling active.*

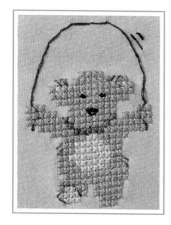

Sporty Top

DESIGN COUNT   80w 34H

FINISHED DESIGN SIZE   7¼ x 3in (18.5 x 8cm)

MATERIALS

* 11-count waste canvas, 9 x 4in (22 x 10cm)
* DMC stranded cottons (floss) listed in the key
* A sports top

1   Position the waste canvas on the front of the top,
ensuring that it is squared up. Tack around the edges and
also diagonally so that the canvas is securely attached to
the one layer of fabric.

2   Stitch the design, following the skipping bear chart on
page 90. Use three strands of stranded cotton (floss) for
cross stitch. Use two strands for backstitch and French
knots.

3   Remove the tacking threads and dampen the canvas
with a cloth. Pull out the strands of waste canvas, one at a
time. Press the finished garment if necessary.

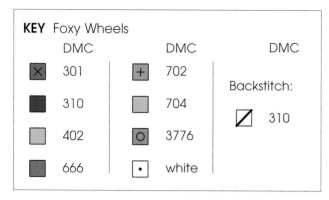

KEY Foxy Wheels		
DMC	DMC	DMC
✕ 301	+ 702	Backstitch:
◼ 310	◻ 704	◹ 310
◻ 402	⊙ 3776	
◼ 666	· white	

Sports Pouch

DESIGN COUNT   50w 67h

FINISHED DESIGN SIZE   3⅝ x 4¾in (9 x 12cm)

MATERIALS

* Green 28-count evenweave, 5 x 20³⁄₈in (13 x 52.5cm)
* DMC stranded cottons (floss) as listed in the key
* Lining fabric, 5 x 20³⁄₈in (13 x 52.5cm)
* Coloured cord, 40in (1m)
* Velcro; sewing thread

1   Orient the evenweave fabric so that the short edges are top and bottom. Stitch the fox, following the foxy wheels chart, so that the base of the design starts ⅝in (1.5cm) from the bottom of the fabric. Use two strands of stranded cotton (floss) for cross stitch and one strand for backstitch.

2   Curve the corners below the design. Sew lining and evenweave together, right sides facing, with a ³⁄₈in (1cm) seam along both long edges and around the curved flap. Turn right side out, turn the raw edges under and handsew the remaining end closed.

3   Sew a strip of Velcro ½in (12mm) down from the hand-sewn end, on the lining side. Fold twice to create a pouch

FOXY WHEELS

6½in (16.5cm) deep with a 6in(15.5cm) flap. Secure the partner piece of Velcro so that it will be inside the pouch.

4   Handsew the side seams of the pouch. Sew the two ends of the cord inside the pouch on either side.

SKIPPING BEAR

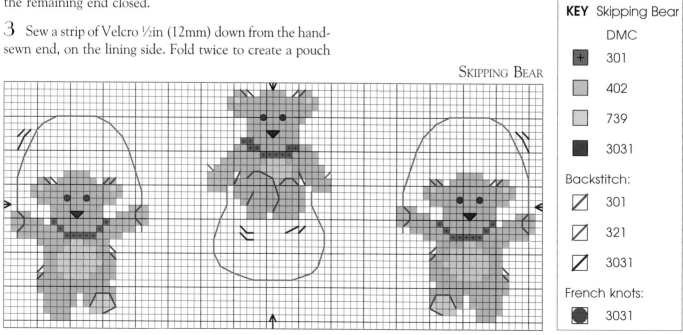

KEY Skipping Bear	
DMC	
+ 301	
◻ 402	
◻ 739	
◼ 3031	
Backstitch:	
◹ 301	
◹ 321	
◹ 3031	
French knots:	
● 3031	

TENNIS CHOOK

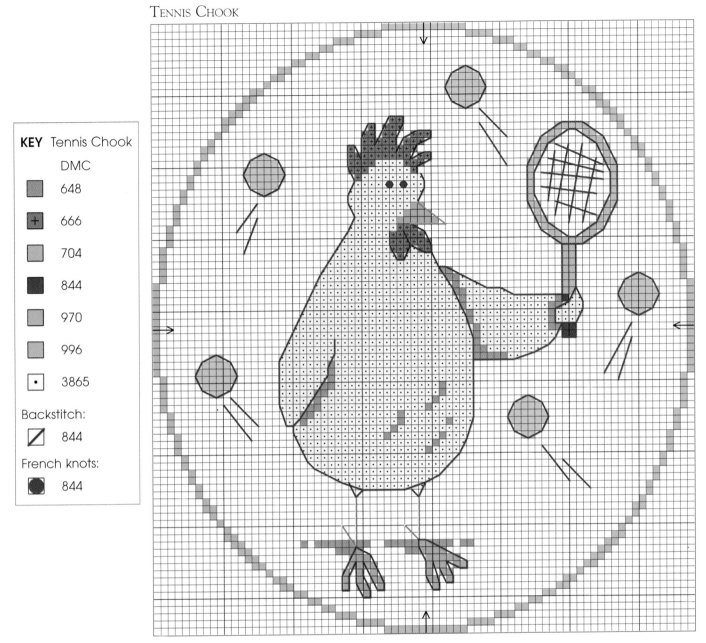

KEY Tennis Chook

DMC

▦	648
+	666
▨	704
▦	844
▨	970
▨	996
⊡	3865

Backstitch:
◩ 844

French knots:
● 844

Racquet Cover

DESIGN COUNT   78w 85h

FINISHED DESIGN SIZE   5½ x 6in (14 x 15cm)

MATERIALS

*   White 14-count Aida, 9 x 9in (23 x 23cm)
*   DMC stranded cottons (floss) as listed in the key
*   Lining fabric, 9 x 9in (23 x 23cm)
*   Strong fabric, approximately 17 x 22in (43 x 55cm)
*   A zipper, 10in (25cm) long
*   Bias binding; sewing thread

1 Stitch the above design in the centre of the Aida fabric. Use two strands of stranded cotton (floss) for cross stitch and one strand for backstitch and French knots.

2 Back the Aida with lining fabric and trim both layers to ⅝in (15mm) around the cross stitch border. Edge the oval-shaped pieces with folded bias binding.

3 Lay your racquet on paper and draw around it to create a generous pattern, marking the handle position. Use this pattern to cut two pieces of strong fabric and sew the cross-stitched panel on the right side of one piece.

4 Cut a strip of strong fabric, ¾in (2cm) wide and 25in (64cm) long. Sew one end of the fabric strip onto the bottom of the closed zipper.

5 Starting at one handle mark, baste the sides of the zipper strip onto the fabric pieces, with wrong sides together. When you reach the other handle mark, hem the end of the strip. Bind the raw edges with folded bias binding.

Doggy Days

×××

Dogs may well be man's best friends but they're also a dab hand in the kitchen. Here are some particularly domesticated doggies at work in the kitchen, cooking up canine cordon bleu.

Apron

DESIGN COUNT	49w 57h
FINISHED DESIGN SIZE	4 x 4⅝in (10 x 11.5cm)

MATERIALS

* Bone 25-count evenweave, 6 x 6in (15 x 15cm)
* DMC stranded cottons (floss) as listed in the key
* Lining fabric, 6 x 6in (15 x 15cm)
* Strong fabric, 25½ x 19½in (65 x 50cm)
* Bias binding; sewing thread

1 Stitch the baking bulldog design on the evenweave fabric, following the chart on page 94. Use two strands for cross stitch and one strand for backstitch.

2 Enlarge the apron pattern on page 109 to three times its current size; note that the dashed line indicates a fold. Cut out a paper template then cut the apron shape from strong fabric. Hem along the base and the straight top and side edges. Sew a length of bias binding along the curves to form a neck loop and ties.

3 Baste the embroidery onto lining fabric, wrong sides facing, and edge with bias binding. Position on the top front of the apron and sew sides and base to form a pocket.

HANDY HOUND

BAKING BULLDOG

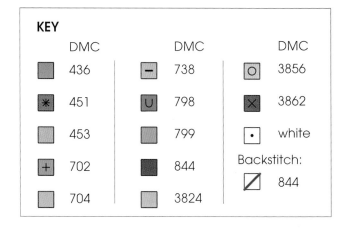

Utensil Holder

DESIGN COUNT   39w 49h

FINISHED DESIGN SIZE   3¹/₈ x 4in (8 x 10cm)

MATERIALS

* Bone 25-count evenweave, 12 x 6in (30 x 15cm)
* DMC stranded cottons (floss) as listed in the key
* A straight-sided jar
* A sheet of acetate (sold with office supplies)
* Double-sided tape

1 Measure the inside circumference and height of your jar; the one in the photograph measures 10 x 6in (25 x 15cm). Cut a piece of acetate 1in (2.5cm) wider and the same height. Cut a piece of evenweave ½in (1.5cm) smaller in both dimensions.

2 Orient the fabric so that the long edges are at top and bottom. Find the centre of the fabric and stitch the design following the handy hound chart above. Use two strands of stranded cotton (floss) for cross stitch and one strand for backstitch and French knots.

3 Apply double-sided tape around the edges on the back of the embroidery and stick onto the acetate. Fit this into the jar and secure the overlapping edge with tape.

KEY

	DMC		DMC		DMC
▦	436	−	738	O	3856
✳	451	U	798	✕	3862
▦	453		799	•	white
+	702		844		Backstitch:
	704		3824	⧄	844

SNIFFER DOG

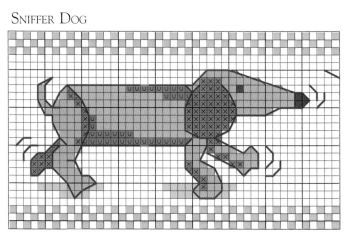

Pot Holder

DESIGN COUNT   45w 45h

FINISHED DESIGN SIZE   3⅝ x 3⅝in (9 x 9cm)

MATERIALS

* Bone 25-count evenweave, 6 x 6in (15 x 15cm)
* DMC stranded cottons (floss) as listed in the key
* Backing fabric, 6 x 6in (15 x 15cm)
* Pre-washed flannel, 6 x 6in (15 x 15cm)
* Bias binding; sewing thread

1 Find the centre of the fabric and stitch the canine cook design following the chart. Use two strands for cross stitch and one strand for backstitch.

2 Arrange the embroidery and backing fabric with wrong sides facing, then place the piece of flannel in between. Baste the three layers together around the edges.

3 Sew a length of folded bias binding around the edges, forming a loop for hanging the pot holder.

CANINE COOK

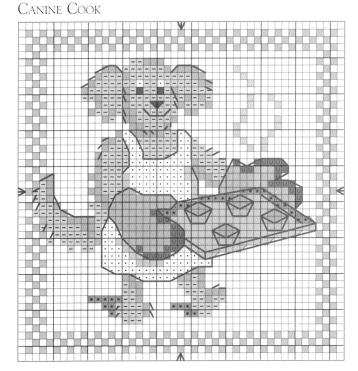

Tea Towel Trim

DESIGN COUNT   125w 26h

FINISHED DESIGN SIZE   10 x 2⅛in (25 x 5.25cm)

MATERIALS

* Bone 25-count evenweave, 3½in (9cm) wide
* DMC stranded cottons (floss) as listed in the key
* A tea towel or hand towel; sewing thread

1 Measure the width of your tea towel or hand towel and cut evenweave fabric 1in (3cm) wider. Stitch the design following the sniffer dog chart below. Use two strands for cross stitch and one strand for backstitch.

2 Turn over the top and bottom of the fabric ¾in (2cm) and press. Sew the strip onto the towel, turning the ends over at either side.

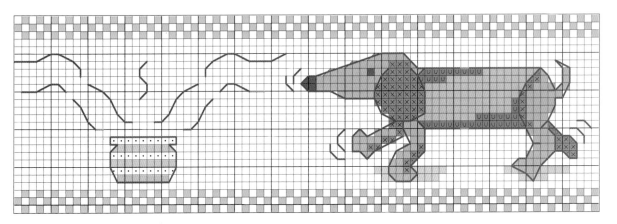

Fridge Magnets

DESIGN COUNT   APPROXIMATELY 40W 40H

FINISHED DESIGN SIZE $2^7/_8$ x $2^7/_8$in (7.5 x 7.5cm)

MATERIALS FOR FOUR FRIDGE MAGNETS

* White 14-count Aida, 10 x 10in (25 x 25cm)
* DMC stranded cottons (floss) as listed in the key
* Stiff white cardboard, 10 x 10in (25 x 25cm)
* Adhesive magnetic tape, 8in (20 cm)
* PVA glue

1 Cut the fabric into four equal squares and stitch a face on each, following the chart. Use two strands for cross stitch.

2 Cut the cardboard into four squares. Spread PVA glue onto one and stick it on the back of one of the cross-stitched faces. Thin some PVA glue with a little water and brush it over the front of the embroidery. Make up the other pieces in the same way and then leave them all to dry and stiffen.

3 Neatly cut ¼in (6mm) around the designs with a strong pair of scissors. Cut four 2in (5cm) pieces of magnetic tape and stick one on the back of each cutout.

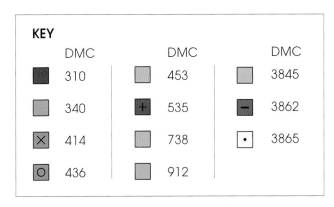

KEY

	DMC		DMC		DMC
■	310	▦	453	▨	3845
▨	340	+	535	–	3862
×	414	▤	738	·	3865
O	436	▦	912		

MAGNETIC MUTTS

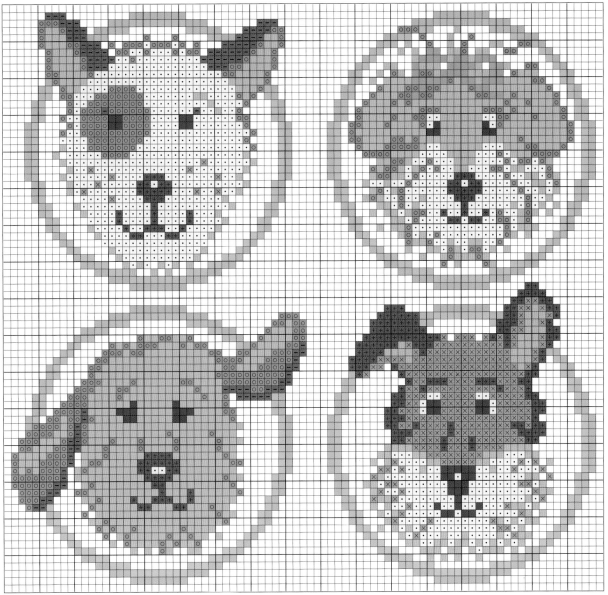

KOALA CAPERS

✕ ✕ ✕

*There's nothing like a picture of
the whole family to produce a
warm, fuzzy feeling. Koala junior
and baby also feature on their own
in smaller snapshots.*

Family Portrait

DESIGN COUNT   174w 140h

FINISHED DESIGN SIZE   12½ x 10in (31.5 x 25.5cm)

MATERIALS

* Rose 28-count evenweave, 20 x 18in (50 x 45cm)
* DMC stranded cottons (floss) as listed in the key
* Framing materials

1 Orient the evenweave fabric so that long edges are top
and bottom. Locate the centre and fit fabric in an embroidery frame if you wish. Stitch the design following the chart
on pages 100-103, using two strands of stranded cotton
(floss) for all cross stitching. Use one strand for backstitch
and French knots.

2 Press the sampler carefully and frame it. There are tips
for framing on page 11.

KEY

	DMC		DMC		DMC
O	208		703		3840
	210	I	725	•	white
	353	X	799		
	355		993		Backstitch:
+	435		3078	╱	208
	437	\	3348	╱	210
L	451	−	3778	╱	310
	453		3799	╱	703

French knots:
● 310

KOALA FAMILY - CHART 1

Baby Cameo

DESIGN COUNT   24w 27h

FINISHED DESIGN SIZE   1¾ x 2in (4.5 x 5cm)

MATERIALS

* White 28-count evenweave, 4 x 4in (10 x 10cm)
* DMC stranded cottons (floss) as listed in the key
* A small gilt frame
* Ribbon

1 Stitch the baby koala design following the chart on the right, using two strands of stranded cotton (floss) for cross stitch and one strand for backstitch.

2 Fit the completed cross stitching in the frame and tie on a ribbon bow.

BABY KOALA

KOALA FAMILY - CHART 2

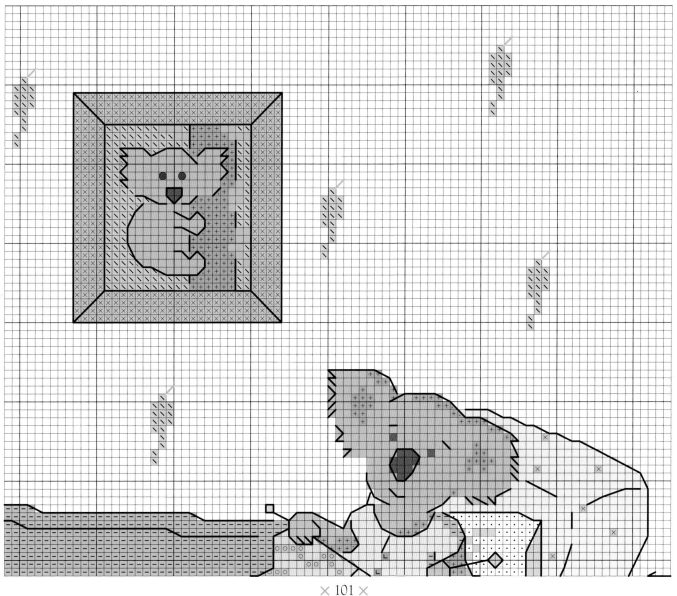

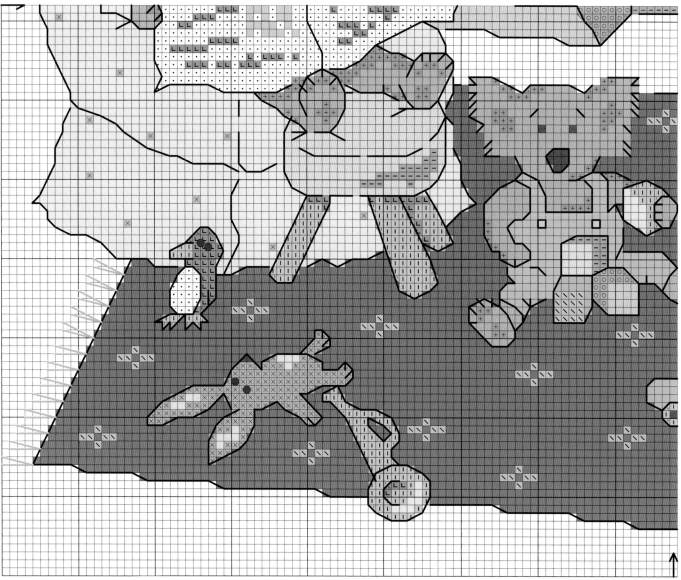

JUNIOR KOALA

Junior Cameo

DESIGN COUNT   32W 35H

FINISHED DESIGN SIZE   2¼ x 2½in (6 x 6.5cm)

MATERIALS

* Yellow 28-count evenweave, 4 x 4in (10 x 10cm)
* DMC stranded cottons (floss) as listed in the key
* A small gilt frame
* Ribbon

1 Stitch the junior koala design following the chart on the left, using two strands of stranded cotton (floss) for cross stitch and one strand for backstitch.

2 Fit the completed cross stitching in the frame and tie on a ribbon bow.

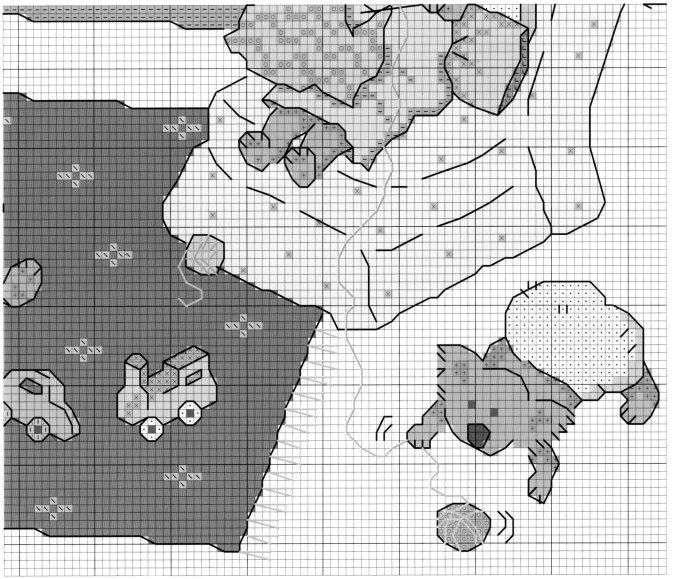

KEY

	DMC		DMC		DMC
O	208		703		3840
	210	I	725	•	white
	353	X	799		Backstitch:
	355		993	/	208
+	435		3078	/	210
	437	\	3348	/	310
L	451	−	3778	/	703
	453		3799		French knots:
					310

CHARMING CHERUBS

✕ ✕ ✕

*What better way to show your affection
than with a few flying cupids? These
cherubs look a little on the mischievous side
but they add a lovely touch to a Valentine,
a fragrant pillow and a delightful
lavender sachet.*

Fragrant Pillow

DESIGN COUNT   29w 28h

FINISHED DESIGN SIZE   2³/₈ x 2¼in (6 x 6cm)

MATERIALS

* Blue 25-count evenweave, 10 x 5in (26 x 13cm)
* DMC stranded cottons (floss) as listed in the key
* Polyester stuffing; floral scent
* Sewing thread; ribbon

1 Cut the fabric in half and stitch the cherub-with-bow
(overleaf) in the centre of a square. Use two strands of
stranded cotton (floss) for cross stitch, except when working with metallic 5283, when you should only use a single
strand. Use one strand for backstitch and French knots.

2 Place the two squares together with right sides facing
and sew a ½in (1cm) seam, leaving a gap for turning. Turn
the pillow right side out.

3 Shake a few drops of floral scent onto some polyester
stuffing and push it into the pillow. Neatly handsew the
opening closed. Decorate with a ribbon bow.

Lavender Sachet

DESIGN COUNT   33w 28h

FINISHED DESIGN SIZE   2⅝ x 2¼in (7 x 6cm)

MATERIALS

* Blue 25-count evenweave, 16 x 6in (40 x 15cm)
* DMC stranded cottons (floss) as listed in the key
* White lining fabric, 16 x 6in (40 x 15cm)
* Sewing thread; ribbon
* Dried lavender

1   Fold the evenweave fabric in half to form an 8 x 6in (20 x 15cm) rectangle. Stitch the cherub-with-harp so that the baseline is 1¼in (3cm) from the folded base. Use two strands of stranded cotton (floss) for cross stitch, except when working with metallic 5283, when you use a single strand. Use one strand for backstitch and French knots.

2   With the stitched design facing inwards, sew the side seams and zigzag all edges to prevent fraying. Turn the bag right side out. Fold over ½in (1cm) at the opening.

3   Fold the white lining fabric in half and sew the side seams. Insert the lining into the bag. Turn the raw edge of the lining opening under and slipstitch it neatly onto the folded linen.

4   Fill the sachet with dried lavender and tie it closed with a ribbon.

Valentine

DESIGN COUNT   35w 26h

FINISHED DESIGN SIZE   2¾ x 2⅛in (7 x 5.5cm)

MATERIALS

* White 25-count evenweave, 5 x 5in (12.5 x 12.5cm)
* DMC stranded cottons (floss) as listed in the key
* Pale pink card, 16½ x 5½in (42 x 14cm)
* Double-sided tape

1   Stitch the cherub-with-heart in the centre of the evenweave fabric. Use two strands of stranded cotton (floss) for cross stitch, except when working with metallic 5283, when you should only use a single strand. Use one strand for backstitch and French knots.

2   Lightly score two lines on the card with a craft knife and fold to create three even panels. Trim a narrow strip off the left panel. With compasses, mark a circle with a diameter of 3½in (9cm) in the centre panel and cut it out.

3   Apply pieces of double-sided tape on the inside of the centre panel. Position the stitched work in the window and stick down the left-hand panel as a backing.

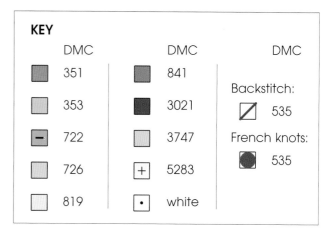

CHERUBIC TRIO

STOCKISTS

✕ ✕ ✕

When writing to any of the following companies, please include a stamped addressed envelope for your reply.

United Kingdom

DMC CREATIVE WORLD LTD
Pullman Road, Wigston, Leicester LE8 2DY
Tel: 0116 281 1040
Cross stitch fabrics and stranded cotton.

FRAMECRAFT MINIATURES LTD
372-376 Summer Lane, Hockley,
Birmingham B19 3QA
Tel: 0121 212 0551
www.framecraft.com
Cross stitch accessories.

SEW AND SO
www.sewandso.co.uk
Tel: 01453 752022
Cross stitch fabrics, stranded cottons and accessories.

USA

THE DMC CORPORATION
Port Kearney Bld, 10 South Kearney, NJ 070732-0650
www.dmc-usa.com
Cross stitch fabrics and stranded cotton.

CHARLES CRAFT
PO Box 1049, Laurinburg, NC 28352
Tel: 910 844 3521
www.charlescraft.com
Cross stitch fabrics and accessories.

Australia

RADDA PTY LTD
PO Box 317, Earlwood NSW 2206
Tel: 02 9559 3088
Distributors of DMC stranded cotton.

IRELAND NEEDLECRAFT PTY LTD
PO Box 1175, Narre Warren MDC Vic 3805
Tel: 03 9702 3222
www.irelandneedlecraft.com.au
Cross stitch fabrics, stranded cottons and accessories.

STADIA PTY LTD
PO Box 281, Paddington NSW 2021
Tel: 02 9328 7900
www.stadia.com.au
Cross stitch fabrics, stranded cottons and accessories.

Charting Software

The designs in this book were created using StitchCraft, an excellent Windows-based software program. For information on this program, please contact:
CRAFTED SOFTWARE
PO Box 78, Wentworth Falls NSW 2782 Australia
Tel: 61 2 4757 3136   Email: mail@stitchcraft.com.au
www.stitchcraft.com.au

THREAD CONVERTER

XXX

DMC stranded cotton (floss) has been used to stitch the designs in this book.
If you wish to use the Anchor brand, refer to this chart for the equivalent shades.
*An * indicates that the Anchor shade has been used more than once.*

DMC	ANCHOR	DMC	ANCHOR	DMC	ANCHOR	DMC	ANCHOR
208	110	535	401	826	161	3747	120
209	109	554	95	841	1082	3752	1032
210	108	611	898*	844	1041	3755	140
211	342	613	831	909	923	3761	928
300	352	644	391	911	205	3766	167
301	1049*	648	900	912	209	3776	1048
310	403	666	46	913	204	3778	1013
317	400	700	228	928	274	3782	388
318	235*	701	227	945	881	3787	904
321	47	702	226	948	1011	3799	236*
334	977	703	238	954	203	3811	1060
340	118	704	256	958	187	3819	278
350	11	721	324	959	186	3823	386
351	10	722	323	963	23	3824	8*
353	8*	725	305	964	185	3826	1049*
355	1014	726	295	970	925	3827	311
402	1047	727	293	975	357	3828	373
413	236*	738	361	976	1001	3838	177
414	235*	739	366	977	1002	3839	176
415	398	741	304	993	1070*	3840	117
422	372	744	301	996	433	3845	1089
433	358	745	300	3021	905*	3846	1090
434	310	746	275	3023	899	3848	1074
435	365	754	1012	3031	905*	3849	1070*
436	363	760	1022	3032	898	3851	186
437	362	797	132	3078	292	3853	1003
444	291	798	146	3325	129	3854	313
451	233	799	145	3340	329	3856	347
453	231	800	144	3341	328	3862	358
469	267	801	359	3347	266	3865	2
470	266*	809	130	3348	264	5283	—
471	265	817	13	3371	382	white	1
472	253	819	271	3607	87		
519	1038	822	390	3609	85		

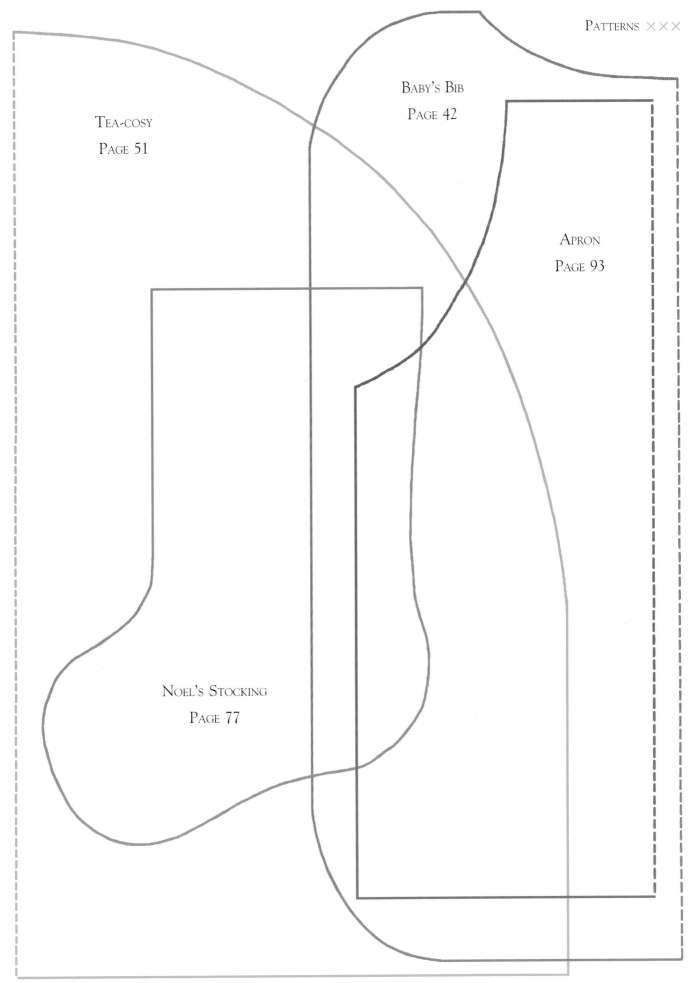

TEA-COSY
PAGE 51

BABY'S BIB
PAGE 42

APRON
PAGE 93

NOEL'S STOCKING
PAGE 77

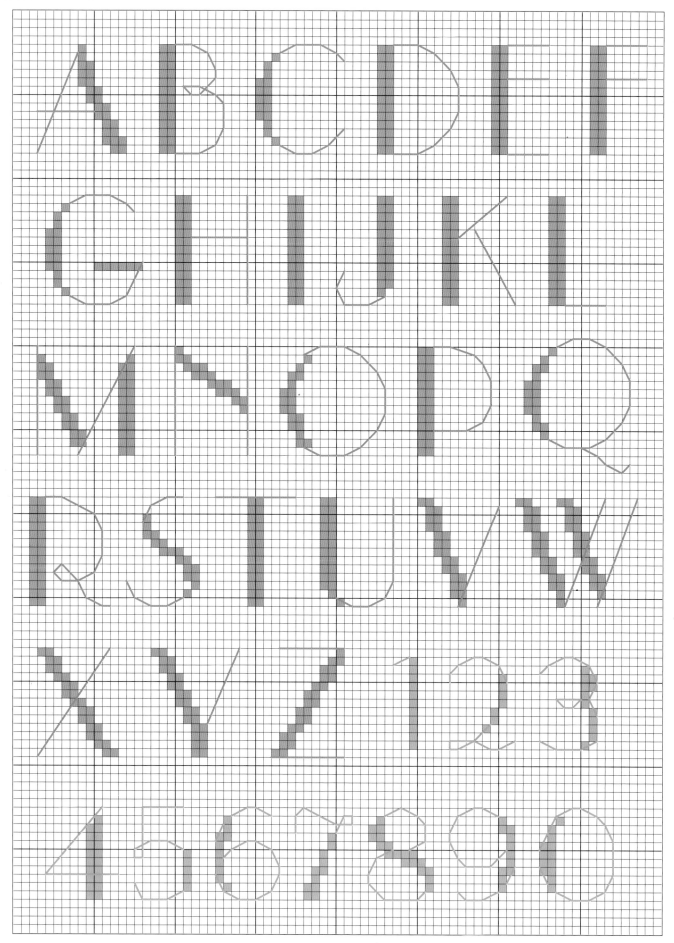

××× INDEX ×××